The History of Schoolboy Football in Blackburn, 1897-1997

by

Rick Grogan

Foreword by Bryan Douglas

(Ex-St.Bartholomew's, Blakey Moor, Blackburn Rovers and England)

A Celebration of One Hundred Years of Organised Football in Blackburn Schools

Blackburn and Darwen Schools' Football Association

© Copyright of the material in this book is held by Rick Grogan.
Published by Blackburn and Darwen Schools' Football Association

ISBN 0 9529503 0 8

Design and layout Mike Clarke
Tel. & Fax 01254 395848

Printed by Nayler the Printers
Tel. 01254 234247/8/9, Fax 01254 383996

Contents

Dedication and Acknowledgements 4

Message from the Chairman, English Schools' F. A. 5

Foreword from Bryan Douglas 6

1897-1914, 'Emmanuel first, the rest nowhere.' 7

1915-1932, 'Pancakes and Ewood Park' 16

          'Arthur's Story' 27

1933-1945, 'Whistles and Wartime Football' 29

1946-1962, 'Please don't pinch the apples' 40

1963-1979, 'The Swinging Sixties & Seventies' 58

1980-1997, 'Parent Power and into the Future' 75

Appendices 94

DEDICATION

Blackburn schools football has come a long way since its beginnings in 1897. Although today's game is a far cry from those early days in terms of equipment, facilities and systems of play, the aim is still very much the same - to provide pupils with a competitive game of soccer involving skill and good sportsmanship.

This book is dedicated to the thousands of teachers who have given their time, expertise and enthusiasm over the past hundred years in order to make this happen.

ACKNOWLEDGMENT

I am indebted to the Lancashire Evening Telegraph and in particular John Napier and Lillian Duffy for allowing many photographs from their library to be reproduced and used in this book.

I would like to thank Howard Talbot Photography for providing several photographs from their files and to Maggie Sims at Blackburn Museum who has also provided some photographs.

The staff at Blackburn Reference Library have been very helpful with requests for use of their materials and finally I would like to thank the many kind individuals who have lent me their own photographs and shared with me their memories of schoolboy football.

Rick Grogan
October 1996

Message from the Chairman of the English Schools' Football Association

In the early 1960s, Blackburn to me meant Bryan Douglas and Ronnie Clayton and the blue and white halved shirts that they used to play in. In my 1960/61 F.A. Book for Boys, Philip Connelly of Coventry went to Blackburn for the day to interview the readers' popular choice, Ronnie Clayton. I'd entered that competition but was unsuccessful like, I suppose, many others.

I vividly remember the 1960 Cup Final when a tiny Wolves winger called Norman Deeley was to score twice after David Whelan suffered a serious injury. I think a bald Derek Dougan also played in that game. Many years later I was to oppose him as he appeared for Kettering in the Southern League. I'd been aware that Blackburn Rovers were one of the original members of the Football League so I looked forward with some anticipation when the first England vs. Holland International at Under-18 Schools level was to be played at Ewood Park. This was back in 1988 before Jack Walker was to have such an effect upon the club.

My memory recalls that Holland won 2-0 and we were lucky to get nil. A certain Brian Roy played for the opposition. The magnificent boardroom and the efficiency and friendliness of the local association who had organised the game have stayed in my mind.

Now the Blackburn and Darwen Schools' Football Association is one of an increasing number of Schools' Football Associations across the country who have or will be celebrating their centenary. What a magnificent achievement this is. Surely only British schoolteachers would contemplate providing a voluntary service to the young over so many generations. Did those founding fathers, and probably a few mothers as well, believe at a time when Victoria was on the throne that their ancestors would still be organising the game 100 years on? Of course they did. They made things to last in those days.

Anyway, congratulations Blackburn and Darwen and here's to the next hundred years.

John Morton
Chairman E.S.F.A.

Foreword from Bryan Douglas

I would like to congratulate Blackburn Schools' Football Association on reaching its century and wish them good luck with its celebrations during 1997.

It seems a very long time ago since I was playing for St. Bartholomew's and then Blakey Moor Boys' School, but I still look back on my schooldays as some of my happiest times in football. The thrill of playing in the Ewood finals were just as great as representing England at international level in later years.

You tend to take teachers for granted when you are at school and it is only when you leave that you appreciate what they do. The teachers which I remember well from my schooldays were Mr. E. Haworth from Blakey Moor who took the football teams and Mr. K. Charnley who looked after the town team when I played.

Once again, congratulations to the B.S.F.A. and may I wish them success for many more years to come.

Bryan Douglas
St. Bartholomew's, Blakey Moor Boys',
Blackburn Rovers and England.

Chapter 1

1897-1914, 'Emmanuel first, the rest nowhere.'

In the year 1897 a group of schoolmasters began to arrange inter-school football games. At that time a local benefactor named Harry Boyle kindly provided a trophy for schoolboy competition. This trophy, known both as the Harry Boyle Cup and as the Blackburn Schoolboys' Cup was a splendid example of craftsmanship. Many people believe that it is possibly the oldest schoolboy trophy in existence, still competed for today.

Harry Boyle himself came from an old and respected Blackburn family. His father, James Boyle, founded a firm that manufactured and sold confectionery and later became involved in local politics. This was not James' only talent because as a result of two marriages he produced some twenty-two children of which Harry was the youngest. By 1897 Harry was also in business and this was described as that of pawnbroker, jeweller, house furnisher and clothier. His premises were to be found at 78 and 80 King Street, Blackburn.

By 1923 Harry had outlived his many brothers and sisters, and his business had expanded. Now, as well as his King Street shops, he had premises at 6 Salford Bridge, Blackburn and at 34 Chapel Street, Chorley.

Right through this period there were many advertisements in the local press about the benefits of shopping at Harry Boyle's and as late as 1930 he was advertising in the Blackburn Rovers programme.

If you are thinking of being MARRIED
THESE HOLIDAYS you cannot do better than SEE

HARRY BOYLE

THE GREAT FURNITURE PROVIDER,
80, KING STREET, BLACKBURN
UNDER THE CLOCK
A HOUSE FIT UP COMPLETE

ON FIRST PAYMENT OF 5/-
and 2s 6d per week afterwards
Call to-day. I am anxious to do business with you.

A FIXTURE FOR LIFE!

is the FURNITURE supplied by

HARRY BOYLE, LTD.

78 & 80 KING STREET and SALFORD BRIDGE
(Just under the Clock)
BLACKBURN

Also at 34 CHAPEL STREET, CHORLEY   Telephone 6516

BLACKBURN ROVERS FIXTURES, 1930-31

The very first cup competition had been organised and was being competed for towards the end of 1897 and the Northern Daily Telegraph of Monday, 22nd November carries the first results of the Harry Boyle Cup. These were as follows:

St. Stephen's 5, St. Paul's 0; Griffin 4, St. Bartholomew's 3; St. Peter's (Mill Hill) 12, Prince St. 0; St. Mary's R.C. 1, St. Peter's 0; St. Thomas's 1, Furthergate 1; St. Alban's 1, Bank Top 1; Mill Hill Catholics 2, St. Luke's 1; Public Higher Grade 7, Wensley Fold 0.

Nearly two months later, the same paper reports on a meeting of the Harry Boyle Challenge Cup Committee of which the principal business was the draw for the 3rd round of the competition. This involved the following schools: Bank Top, St. Peter's R.C., St. Anne's, St. Matthew's, St. Stephen's, St. Thomas's. St. Peter's, Lower Darwen, Emmanuel, St. Philip's, St. Andrew's, Parish Higher Grade, Moss St., Mayson St., Mill Hill, Park Road, Public Higher Grade and St. Joseph's.

The Harry Boyle Cup donated to the Blackburn Schools by local businessman Harry Boyle in 1897.

Also at this meeting a protest was heard from Moss Street School which alleged that Mayson Street had played an ineligible player named Walmsley and the committee ordered the match to be replayed. A protest by Christ Church against Parish Higher Grade for a similar offence was dismissed.

The first Harry Boyle Cup Final was between Parish Higher Grade and Mill Hill Congregational School, and took place on Shrove Tuesday, 22nd February 1898 at Ewood Park. Parish won the game by two goals to nil, but there was a protest from the opposition about the eligibility of one of the Parish team.

A special meeting of the Harry Boyle Cup Committee was held on 2nd March 1898 with Mr.J.Lewis in the chair (The same John Lewis who was a founder member of Blackburn Rovers). A protest from Mill Hill was read regarding a player from Parish, one John Hartley Birtwell, whom it was alleged was over age. A certificate of birth was produced from which it appeared that while Parish School believed Birtwell to have been born on the 31st October 1883, he was actually born on the first of that month. The claim that he was over age was upheld and the match was ordered to be replayed. In the opinion of the meeting, Parish School had acted in perfectly good faith in playing Birtwell.

The replay took place on Saturday, 26th March at Ewood Park with admission for adults 3d.; boys 1d. and the Grand Stand 3d. extra. In bleak weather before a poor attendance Parish Higher Grade again beat Mill Hill, this time by three goals to nil. Thus Parish became the first winners of the Harry Boyle Cup. Their team that day was: Green in goal, Howarth, Culshaw (backs), Hamer, Bunyon, Wilson (half backs), Stott, Farnworth, Ainsworth, Cooper, Ashton (forwards).

Incidentally, after the original game there had been another match between Blackburn Day School teachers and Burnley Day School teachers with the Blackburn teachers featuring William Townley on the left wing. Townley, a schoolmaster by profession, had played 123 games for the Rovers in the 1880s and early 1890s and gained two international caps as well as two F.A.Cup Final Winner's Medals. He was also the first man to score a hat-trick in an F.A.Cup Final.

On Friday, 1st April 1898 the Harry Boyle Challenge Cup Committee met again at Kirtlan's Restaurant, Ainsworth Street, with the principal business being the distribution of the proceeds of the cup-ties to charities. The sum to be divided was £44-1s-0d of which the Teachers' Orphan Fund was voted £20 (as per agreement), Blackburn Orphanage and All Saints' Ragged School received £5 each, the Deaf and Dumb Society received £2, the North East Lancs. Blind Society and 'Pearson's' Fresh Air Fund one guinea each.

Mr. Mark Russell said that anyone giving a donation of £5 or upwards became a life member of the Teachers' Charity Organisation and that four of the committee, H.Boyle (the promoter of the competition). F.Woodhouse, W.Chadwick and N.Kisielowski, were chosen as members. Local benevolent and orphan funds continued to benefit from the proceeds of the Harry Boyle Cup for many years to come. Finally the meeting passed a vote of thanks to the Blackburn Rovers F.C. Committee for having lent their ground for a number of the matches.

For the next five years the competition was dominated by Emmanuel School and after their third consecutive victory in 1901, Emmanuel had earned the right to keep the trophy for all time. Fortunately, especially for the many subsequent winners, Emmanuel returned the cup to the Association for further competition. To mark this action, Harry Boyle presented the school with a silver shield to keep in recognition of their achievement.

After this victory in 1901, the winning Emmanuel team drove from Ewood Park in triumph back to school in a horse-drawn wagonette, holding the cup for all to see. It appears that the team also rubbed salt into the defeated teams wounds by touring the Moss Street neighbourhood as well. Emmanuel had beaten Moss Street by five goals to one in the final.

It is interesting to note that a member of this winning team, Mr. Herbert Hartley, recalled many years later that equipment and facilities were very different then. For example, very few boys had boots in those days and, as clogs were banned, most played in shoes. However, for the Final itself, some boys nailed studs to their

Sunday best shoes and played in those. Mr. Hartley remembered also that Town team games were organised at this time and he represented Blackburn in a fixture versus Lancaster. The boys travelled to Lancaster by train for just a few pence.

Emmanuel's monopoly on the Harry Boyle Cup was finally broken in 1904 when St. Stephen's won the trophy. Rowland Ogden, a member of the St. Stephen's winning team, recalled some years ago that they beat Moss Street in the semi-finals thanks to a goal scored by Albert Chippendale. For the final, Mr. Ogden said that they worked hard under the direction of Mr.F.Parkinson, who was pupil teacher at that time and they beat Lower Darwen St. James' (Bolton Road) 2-1 despite Jimmy Threlfall missing a penalty.

However, Emmanuel were back winning in 1906 and three years later, in the Blackburn Weekly Telegraph of February, 1909, after Emmanuel had won the Harry Boyle Cup for the seventh time in the first twelve years of its existence, one reporter wrote, *"Once upon a time it was a case of Emmanuel first and the rest nowhere, but no longer have they the almost certain assurance of victory that they once had."*

During this spell of supremacy Emmanuel had three teachers who had a great influence on the team. Mr. Lupton, Headmaster from 1882 until his death in 1913, took a tremendous interest in the boys and their football. Mr. Charles Houlden was Assistant Master and Mr. Kisielowski was Pupil Teacher and both these devoted their time and energies to the football teams. In fact Mr. Houlden was Secretary of the Blackburn Schools Football Association from 1901-1929 and his family today

Emmanuel at Ewood Park in 1906 where they became winners of the Harry Boyle Cup for the sixth time. Mr.Houlden and Mr.Lupton are on the back row, and note the Ewood changing rooms in the background.

The Emmanuel School Team which won the Harry Boyle Cup in 1901-02. At the front is the Harry Boyle Shield, given to the school in recognition of their three consecutive wins.
On the back row is Charles Houlden (2nd from left) who was Secretary of the Blackburn Schoolboys' Football Association from 1901 to 1929. Mr. Lupton, the headmaster, is 5th from the left and on the extreme right is Mr. Kisielowski, the trainer of the team.

still have the display cabinet with which he was presented on his retirement. Mr. Kisielowski was the trainer of the team and when possible he would arrange matches against older boys of around fifteen, most of whom worked in local mills.

Another reason for the success of Emmanuel at that time could have been that the team were in the big money class. When they won their games it worked out at 6d., 3d. from the headmaster and 3d. from the assistant master, plus 2d. from Mr. Kisielowski for all those who scored goals.

Within a very short space of time the Harry Boyle Cup had created a great deal of interest and Blackburn Rovers were generously allowing Ewood Park to be used for the Final - a gesture which they repeated for the next eighty years or so. Traditionally, Shrove Tuesday was fixed as the date for the semi-finals or finals and a crowd numbering into thousands would make their way to the ground.

In the early part of the century schoolboy football was mentioned on the same pages as the professional game. In a report in the Blackburn Weekly Telegraph of February 1909 under the title *'The Fight for the Schoolboys' Cup'*. It says; *'All the talk in the football world just now is of cups and cup-ties, for this is the season of the year when the more prosaic league tournament is eclipsed in interest by the concentrated excitement of cup encounters. The enthusiasm for cup-ties, as far as* local followers of football are concerned, received a drenching douche on Saturday, when the visions of a return to the ancient triumphs of the Rovers that some of us had been cherishing were extinguished for another long twelve months by the men of Manchester.' (Rovers had lost 6-1 in the 3rd round of the F.A.Cup to United the previous week)

The report goes on to say, *'But there is another cup yet to be fought for, the semi-finals of which were played at Ewood Park on Tuesday - the Blackburn Schoolboys' Cup, the yearly competition which has become an established attraction in the town.'*

The report of 1909 gives an interesting insight into football at this time and schoolboy players compare very favourably with their professional counterparts. It says of the schoolboy final that, *'As a matter of fact it is football and nothing but football that one sees in these games. There are none of those mean little tricks adopted to take an unfair advantage of an opponent when the referee's back is turned which are too often seen in professional games, nor is there the least suspicion of any player showing a disinclination to exert himself as is also to be found frequently in the case of players in teams of a far higher reputation.'*

It goes on, *'In the average Blackburn boy there is a wonderful amount of enthusiasm for the winter game. Add to that a very considerable amount of skill and cleverness in the niceties of the positions and you get an idea of the average player in one of these school teams. Take eleven such players and imagine a well-nigh perfect under-standing and you have a combination such as is generally victorious in the Schoolboys' Cup Final. And these annual games for the Cup do not suffer by comparison with matches which attract tens of thousands of people. Indeed a ten thousand 'gate' has been known before now when the final has been played.'*

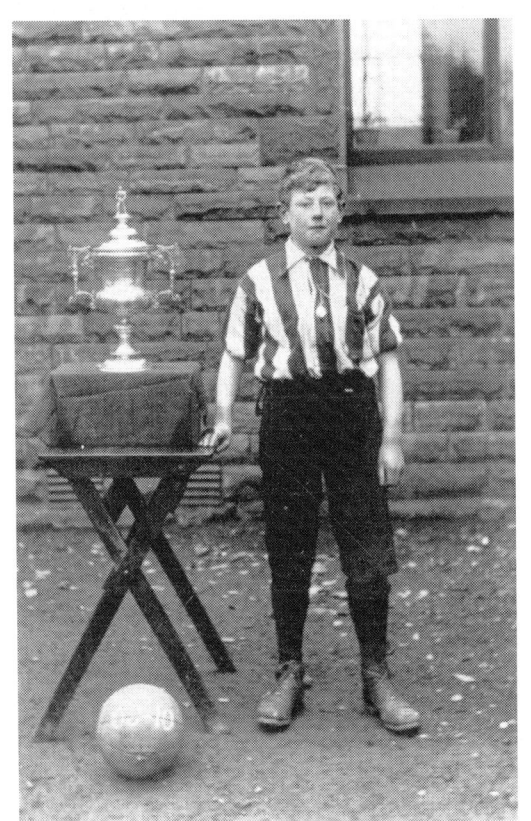

A proud member of the St. Stephen's School Team with the Harry Boyle Cup in 1910. This was the second and last time they won the Schoolboys' Cup, having won previously in 1904.

Note the ball and the boots, but also the gold winners medal pinned on his shirt!

Winners 1911

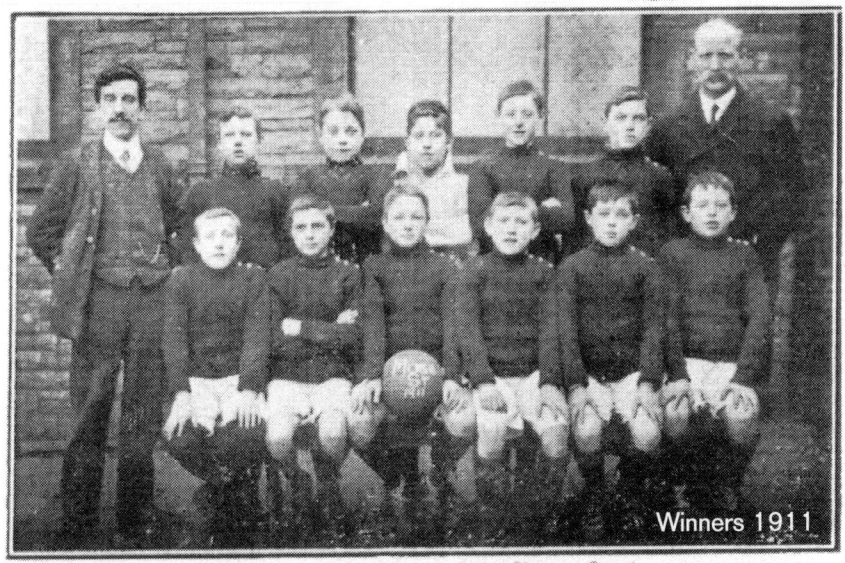

(Winners, Blackburn Schoolboys' Cup)

Standing, left to right—Mr A Sauvain (coach) C Barton E King J Duckworth J Murray J Haworth and Mr H Ashton (headmaster) Sitting—T Boardman Wm Shaw Bert Wilkinson (captain) Wm Walton Hy Harrison and A Stewart

MOSS STREET.

The following year, 1910, the Blackburn Times reports, *'The schoolboy matches have an attraction for Blackburn people and rightly so. For one thing it is wise to encourage healthy sport amongst boys and, for another, it is really enjoyable to watch these lads play in what to them is very serious football.*

Quite 6,000 spectators, adults and juveniles, were present at Ewood Park on Tuesday afternoon to witness the semi-final ties of the Schoolboys' Cup.'

St. Stephen's and Christ Church won through to the final which was played on Saturday, 19th February at Ewood. St. Stephen's won by 5 goals to nil and *'nobody will deny that the trophy was captured by the better side, whose football was of an excellent quality. Blackwell distributed the ball with rare judgement and also had the distinction of registering 3 goals.'*

In fact, each year local newspaper reports enthused about the schoolboy matches and the football that was played. It was often described as wholehearted, clean and full of endeavour as well as skilful and enjoyable. Nor was it just a game between the schools involved, but an event that aroused widespread interest in the town. Even though football was a popular spectator sport, why else would several thousand supporters go along to watch these games? Schoolboy football was held in high esteem and the Harry Boyle Competition was a big attraction to many people in the area.

Another development in the early part of the century which should be mentioned was the formation of the English Schools' Football Association in 1904. Although

CHRIST CHURCH
Winners of Blackburn Schoolboys' Cup.

EMMANUEL SCHOOLBOYS, BLACKBURN, 1913-14.
Winners of the Blackburn Elementary Schools' F.A. Cup for the eighth time.

Darwen were one of the original members, it was not until 1906 that Blackburn were affiliated and entered the English Schools Knockout Competition. After beating Bury 3-0 in a replay, Blackburn Boys went out to Bolton 3-2, again after a replay. The members of the Blackburn Schools Football Committee at this time included the Chairman, Mr. H. Ashton, of 3 Edgeware Road and the Secretary for the English Cup Competition was Mr. W. Alston of 156 St. James' Road.

Although the Town teams did not do particularly well, the Harry Boyle Cup continued to flourish and, by the outbreak of the First World War, Emmanuel had won their eight Schoolboys' Cup Final out of seventeen attempts. The other winners in this period were: Parish Higher Grade (1898), St. Stephen's (1904 & 1910), Moss Street (1905, 1907 & 1911), St. Philip's (1908) and Christ Church (1912 & 1913).

It is sad to note that many of the footballers who had taken part in the early Harry Boyle Competitions would lose their lives in the war.

But the Competition went on and another school began to dominate - Parish Higher Grade.

WANT TO KNOW THE SCORE?

Get the paper that's top of the league for the coverage of sport.

LANCASHIRE EVENING **Telegraph**

It's number one for all local and national sport.

Chapter 2
1915-1932, 'Pancakes and Ewood Park'

During the early part of this period, Parish Higher Grade were the most successful school in the Harry Boyle Cup winning in 1916, 1917, 1919, 1920 and again in 1921 and 1922 when the school was known as the Church of England Central School. Parish had won the very first competition in 1898 so had now been successful on seven occasions.

Parish were favourites to win the cup in 1915 mainly because of their league record which read: Played 6, won 6, lost 0, drawn 0, goals for 59, goals against 0, points 12.

However, they were beaten by three goals to one by Moss Street in the semi-final. In the other semi-final Norfolk Street (St. Aidan's) had beaten Bank Top. Both these games had been played at Ewood Park on Shrove Tuesday when the gate receipts had been £20. There must have been a crowd of a few thousand when one remembers that admission was only a few pence and there were 240 pennies to a pound in those days. Moss Street went on to win the Cup, but Parish were back in the final the following year.

The semi-finals for 1916 were again held on Shrove Tuesday and the scene was well described in the local press. *'Blackburn schoolboys had a gala at Ewood Park on "Pancake" Tuesday and in spite of a snowstorm they made the welkin ring with their merry shouts.'* The report goes on to describe the crowd and atmosphere. *'The lads were fierce partisans - they yelled for their school and extended no mercy for the fallen. Caps were bedecked with the colours of their favourites, hundreds of rosettes were sported, partly coloured umbrellas were carried and flags waved vigorously. Add to that the deafening shouts of juvenile spectators, the roll of kettle drums, the blare of bugles, snow coming down steadily and 22 lads playing as if for their lives and the picture is complete.*

In addition a number of wounded soldiers enjoyed the fun immensely and the teachers entered thoroughly into the spirit of the occasion.'

The actual football resulted in wins for Parish Higher Grade and Higher Elementary School who met in the final on Saturday 18th March in front of a large crowd.

'Both elevens were enthusiastically received and a spirited contest witnessed. Parish won the game 1-0 with a penalty scored by Hope, who had been a particularly prominent player and who was carried off shoulder high at the end of

the game. Also, like good sportsmen, each side gave three hearty cheers for the other.' Right from their early days in 1898, Parish Higher Grade were under the guidance of teacher Mr. F.S.Horsfall who was trainer and responsible for much of their success.

The Town team of 1916 was made up of ten players from the Parish Higher Grade and the Higher Elementary Schools with one boy coming from Moss Street and one from Griffin. The team did very well in the English Schools Competition beating Barrow 8-1, Lancaster 6-0 and Crewe 7-0 reaching the semi-final of Division VI before losing 3-1 to Liverpool Boys at Anfield.

However, one of the team, Ronald Rodden of Parish Higher Grade, was selected to play for England Schoolboys in the match against Wales at Burnden Park, Bolton, on Saturday 15th April. Rodden, a right back, was described in the local press as a fearless tackler, a judicious feeder and a skilful defender and, if he produced his school form, the Welsh left winger would have an unhappy time. England won the game 2-1 and Ronald Rodden became the first Blackburn schoolboy to gain an international cap.

At this time there was no County Association. This was formed in 1920 as the result of a meeting held at the Lancashire Football Association offices in Ainsworth Street, Blackburn, on the 2nd January. Nine towns were represented at the meeting and rules for the County Cup Competition were formulated. Seven towns: Barrow, Blackburn, Bolton, Burnley, Liverpool, Manchester and Preston, were to take part in the competition in its first season.

During the 1920s Blackburn had some experienced and dedicated teachers looking after the Town teams. These included F.S.Horsfall. a teacher at Parish Higher Grade since the 1890s, Ben Aspinall, appointed headmaster at Emmanuel in 1922 where he remained for the next thirty years and Mr.T.Ormerod who taught at St. Aidan's and who was still involved with football there in 1947. In addition there was Norman Smith, a teacher at Park Road School, who helped with the Town teams and W.E.Bradley, a long serving member of the Football Committee.

Perhaps one of the best and strongest Town teams came together in 1923 when Blackburn won the Lancashire County Cup Competition. From the original seven towns that took part in 1920, there were now thirty five local Associations affiliated to the Lancashire Schools F.A. Although beaten 2-1 by Liverpool Boys at Griffin Ground in the English Schools Competition, Blackburn were unstoppable in the Lancashire Cup. In the second round they beat Warrington 11-0 at Griffin with Duxbury (Accrington Road School) scoring six; in round three they hammered Dalton-on-Furness by nine goals to nil with Bilsborough (Bank Top) scoring four goals and Duxbury three. By this time there was great interest in the semi-final played at Ewood on Thursday 5th April 1923, against Manchester Boys. Manchester had won the Lancashire Cup for the previous two years and included in their team Hugh McLenahan, their international player. Blackburn eventually won the game by two goals to one and were described as a very big team that showed an excellent understanding and were very fast in attack and defence. Saturday 12th May, again at Ewood, was the day of the final in which Blackburn met Eccles Boys. On a big

The Blackburn Team before their Lancashire Cup Semi-final against Manchester Boys at Ewood Park - Thursday 5th April 1923. *Back row from the left*: Mr. Norman Smith, Mr. W. E. Bradley, E.Smith (C.E.Central), Mr. R. B. Chase of Burnley (Chairman of the L.S.F.A.), J.Fisher (C.E.Central), Mr. F. S. Horsfall, Mr. B. Aspinall. *Middle*: E.Earnshaw (Griffin), P.Duxbury (Accrington Road), H.Bilsborough (Bank Top), F.Marsden (Audley Range), H.Walsh (Blakey Moor), F.Hargreaves (C.E.Central). *Front*: H.Readett (Blakey Moor), T.Haworth (Emmanuel), H.Chambers (C.E.Central).

The Blackburn Schoolboys Squad with officials of the Blackburn Schools' F.A. and the Lancashire County Elementary Schools' F.A. Cup, 1923.

pitch, with a strong wind, Eccles were rushed off their feet, but Blackburn only won by a solitary goal which came from Chambers, the Blackburn centre half. He scored with a long shot just before the interval.

Not surprisingly five of this team, Hargreaves, Bilsborough, Duxbury, Earnshaw and Fisher gained County honours in 1923. The Cup was presented to the Blackburn captain by R.Watson, Vice-President of the L.F.A. who remarked that what pleased him greatly was to see the game played without any sign of unfairness. He advised the boys to let this ever be a feature of their play, so that not only would it be a great satisfaction to themselves but it would help to purge the game of its objectionable aspects.

The 1920s were also a time of rapid development and expansion of schoolboy football in Blackburn. In 1919 the Blackburn Association had been presented with a new trophy, the Thornton Shield, by one of His Majesty's Inspectors of Schools, so now there were two competitions, with the Thornton Shield for boys under scholarship age.

The first time that the two Schoolboy Finals were played together was on Saturday 8th May 1920 at Ewood Park. According to local newspaper reports, *'keen rivalry and good football were equally prominent features when the two*

BANK TOP, WINNERS OF THE THORNTON SHIELD.
Back Row (left to right): Mr. T. Holden (headmaster), Miss A. Horsfall, Mr. C. Houlden (hon. secretary, B.S.F.A.).
Middle Row: J. Chadwick, H. Bilsborough, F. Sanderson, T. Booth, H. Smith.
Front Row: J. Clegg, W. Murray, W. Greaves, H. Ross (captain), C. Lee, W. Duxbury, A. Hargreaves, J. Greaves.

competitions in connection with the Blackburn Schoolboys' Association were both decided. There was a good attendance of parents and friends as well as other persons interested in football. The gate receipts for the games were allocated to the Blackburn War Memorial Fund.'

The two finalists for the Thornton Shield were Mill Hill C.E. School and Bank Top who had beaten Blakey Moor 6-0; St. Andrew's 11-0; St. Stephen's 1-0; and Christ Church 2-1 on the way to the final. Local reports describe the match as *'...a ding-dong struggle, in which both sides strove to score in turn, the attempts being interspersed with hard struggles in mid-field. The winning goal followed a corner, which resulted in a scrimmage in the Mill Hill goalmouth and Walton putting the ball out of the goalkeeper's reach.'* The game resulted in a win for Bank Top by this solitary goal, and they became the first winners of the Thornton Shield.

The finalists for the Harry Boyle Cup were Moss Street and Parish Higher Grade, both renowned cup fighters. Moss Street, previous winners on four occasions, had defeated St. Stephen's in the semi-final by two goals to nil in which *'B.King, the diminutive Moss Street centre half, was a fearless tackler and plied the forwards in a skilful manner, opening out the game.'*

Parish, on the other hand, had defeated St. Oswald's 10-0; Higher Elementary 2-0; Emmanuel 1-0; and Bank Top 4-0 in the other semi-final. Also, according to newspaper reports, *'The Parish team have had the advantage of many interesting players, including D.Suttie, son of Tommy Suttie, the Rovers celebrated full back; Chad Townley, son of W.J.Townley the Rovers international and Harry and Robert Crompton, sons of Bob Crompton the present Rovers captain.'*

After a goalless first half, Parish took control and eventually won by three goals to nil, these coming from Hargreaves, Suttie and Slater. Parish had won their sixth Harry Boyle Final and had, on the way, won five games, scoring twenty goals and conceding none.

As well as the Thornton Shield introduced in the 1919-1920 season, there were two new cup competitions introduced in 1923-1924. These were for secondary aged pupils in what was known as a Central Schools Competition. The two trophies were the Stanworth Cup and the Forrest Cup, the latter donated by Alderman J.W. Forrest O.B.E., who later became Sir William Forrest.

Both of these new cups were very much dominated by the new Blakey Moor School They won the Stanworth Cup in 1924, 1925, 1927 and 1928, and the Forrest Cup in 1924, 1925, 1926, 1928 and 1929. Add to this Blakey Moor's success in the Thornton Shield in 1922 and 1923 and the school was winning at least one trophy every year and quite often two.

The only occasion Blakey Moor did not win the Forrest Cup in the 1920s was in 1927 when they were beaten by the Grammar School in the final. This was the first ever success by the Grammar School in the local Blackburn football competitions and it came on the 14th May at Ewood Park. Incidentally, this winning Grammar School team featured a young George Armistead who was later to teach locally and serve on the Football Committee for many years.

Blakey Moor Central School were therefore the most successful school in the

The Blackburn Grammar School Under-14 Team, Winners of the Forrest Cup, 1926-27. *Back row from the left*: L.Bamford, W.S.Holden, Mr.B.A.Workman, J.D.Forbes, W.Robinson. *Middle*: A.R.Riley, G.Kennedy, H.Spink, G.Armistead, J.Allsup. *Front*: S.Thompson, F.Haydock, J.Lee.

The Blakey Moor Junior Team who beat Bangor Street by two goals to one to win the Thornton Shield. *Back row from left*: Mr.D.S.Miller, J.Ramsden, H.Readett, Fred Haworth, R.Bradburn, Mr.H.Rydings. *Middle*: Percy Taylor, Cecil Cross, H.Parker, J.Smalley, J.Lowe, R.Delaney. *Front*: W.Hartley and W.Almond.

The Blakey Moor Senior Team who beat C.E.Central by four goals to one to win the Harry Boyle Cup. This picture shows the headmaster, Mr. H.W. Boddy, in the centre at the back and some of the players who played in both teams - W. Almond and Harold Readett.

1920s. In 1923 they did the 'double' with the senior team winning the Harry Boyle Cup and the juniors the Thornton Shield. Harold Readett, who played for both teams, was also a member of the Blackburn Town team that won the County Cup in 1923 and later played for both the Rovers and then Burnley Reserves. He later looked after the 'A' teams at Blackburn and ended up as chief scout for the Rovers in the late 1950s and 1960s.

A newspaper report from the 1920s perhaps best describes the feeling for the Blackburn Schools' Cup competitions when it states *'To the average Blackburn schoolboy, Shrove Tuesday means pancakes and Ewood Park. The enthusiasm as the best school teams in the town play for the Harry Boyle Cup never seems to decline.'*

The 1920s also saw some new winners of the Harry Boyle Cup. In 1923 Blakey Moor won for the first time, Park Road Congregational won for the one and only time in 1926 and St. Aidan's won twice in 1927 and 1928. St. Peter's R.C. School won the Cup for the first time in 1930 beating Moss Street 2-1 after extra-time, but Moss Street won the Cup in the next two seasons to record their seventh success in the competition.

This victory in 1932 was to be the last for Moss Street, who defeated their old enemy, Emmanuel, by one goal to nil, a goal scored by Hesmondhalgh described as, *'a tricky little inside left and the cleverest player in the match.'* This victory also coincided with the last occasion on which they had Mr. James Kenyon as headmaster. This gentleman, who retired in March of that year, had done great work for schoolboy football and had led his Moss Street boys to many successes.

The Blackburn Team of 1920 pictured in the Blackburn Times of the 24th January.

St. Aidan's (Norfolk Street F.C.), winners of the Thornton Shield, 1921.

Blakey Moor Central School, the very first winners of the Forrest Cup in 1923/24 season.

23

Emmanuel School, winners of the Harry Boyle Cup in 1925. Ben Aspinall, headmaster, is standing fourth from the left, next to Mr.Ettock. Canon Samuel with the team's lucky mascot is in the centre at the front.

Park Road Con-gregational School, winners in 1926, defeating Moss Street two goals to one in the final at Ewood Park.

St.Aidan's, winners in 1928, defeating Moss Street 4-0, goals scored by Taylor (2), Campbell and Ormandy. The out-standing player was Taylor, grandson of the famous Nat. Walton, a winner of three Cup Final medals with Rovers (1886, 1890 & 1891). The cup was presented to the captain, Colin Campbell, by the Rovers F.A. Cup winning captain of that year, Harry Healless.

St.Aidan's School won the Thornton Shield in 1925. The teacher on the left, Mr. T. Ormerod, became headmaster and appeared with winning teams as late as 1947.

The Moss Street Team who were runners-up in the Harry Boyle Cup Final of 1930. They were beaten 2-1 by Mill Hill St. Peter's after extra-time. Moss Street went on to win the Cup in the following two years.

Emmanuel School, winners of the Thornton Shield in 1931.

Arthur's Story

One of the most colourful accounts of the many schoolboy finals appeared in the Blackburn Times on 18th March 1933, describing the final of the Forrest Cup the previous Thursday. It read: *'There is a centre forward in Blackburn called Arthur; his other name is Chatburn. Arthur stands every bit of 4 feet $6^{1}/_{2}$ inches tall, hardly big enough to cause trouble one might say. But Arthur is a decided power for good and evil. On Thursday night the hearts of over 300 boys were in their boots because of Arthur, while as many other lads were in the seventh heaven of delight just for the same small reason.*

Arthur is the dashing leader of the C.E.Central School team who, in the final of the Forrest Cup at Ewood, beat rivals Blakey Moor Central School by 6 goals to 2.

Arthur's modest contribution to victory was three goals and a large share in another.

He executed his disturbing skills by getting a goal almost at once. When his side were a goal down, Arthur rolled up his sleeves and cheekily scored an equaliser. He next crashed the ball against the crossbar for a colleague to take the easiest of chances from the rebound.

Then a Blakey Moor defender committed the unpardonable sin of fouling Arthur in the penalty area. That was simply inviting trouble. Arthur scowled furiously, hitched up his pants and exacted retribution with a penalty goal.

But for the final whistle Arthur would probably have been goal-getting yet.'

For the record, J.Parker and J.Parkinson scored for Blakey Moor, while, as well as Arthur, K.Parkinson, W.Murray and W.Yates scored for C.E.Central.

Tel: Blackburn (01254) 582944

GIBSONS SPORTS LTD

17 NEW MARKET STREET

BLACKBURN BB1 7DR

The successful C. E. Central School and Arthur with the Forrest Cup at his feet. *Back row from the left*: Mr. G. H. Smithies, Jimmy Bentley, Jimmy Walsh, Mr. A. Walker (Headmaster), Tommy Harral, John Farren, Mr.C.Walton. *Middle*: Bill Murray, Ken Parkinson, Arthur Chatburn, Bill Yates, Bill Walkden. *Front*: Jack Chew, Jim Fish, Jack Farnworth, Albert Morley.

There are many interesting characters on the above photograph. The headmaster in the centre of the back row was known affectionately as Mr. 'Daddy' Walker, while the teacher on the left was George Smithies, an England amateur international who also played for Preston North End. The other teacher on the right was Clarence Walton, later to become headmaster of Blakey Moor Boys School.

Eight of this squad were in the successful C.E.Central team which beat Bangor Street 5-0 in the final of the Stanworth Cup at Ewood Park on the 13th May 1933. Jack Chew played about 247 games for Burnley, including the 1947 Cup Final at Wembley.

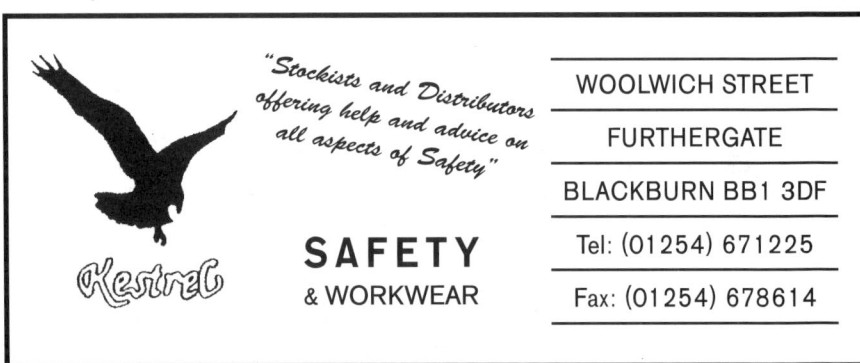

Kestrel

"*Stockists and Distributors offering help and advice on all aspects of Safety*"

SAFETY & WORKWEAR

WOOLWICH STREET

FURTHERGATE

BLACKBURN BB1 3DF

Tel: (01254) 671225

Fax: (01254) 678614

Chapter 3
1933-1945, 'Whistles and Wartime Football'

As early as 1931 there was a suggestion that the sporting activities run by teachers on behalf of children should be brought together into one organisation. However, it was not until Friday, 30th June 1933 that there was a meeting of teachers interested in this idea. At this meeting, held at the Technical College, was born the Blackburn Schools' Athletic Association which would control the affairs of football, athletics, swimming and girls' games.

Although each of these sports had its own elected committee, they would send representatives to the Central Council meetings of the Association and produce an annual report outlining the events of the previous year.

The first Football Committee consisted of Messrs. Aspinall, Bradley, Fish, Duerden, Ormerod, Riding and Sullivan. By the end of the year, Richard Blackburn was Honorary Secretary of the Football Committee and he wrote the very first Annual Report. This was the beginning of a long and valuable association between Richard Blackburn and the Football Committee. He served as Secretary and Chairman for many years. In 1953 he was appointed Vice-President of Blackburn Referees' Association and in 1959 he was nominated and elected as a Life Member of Lancashire Schools' Football Association. He was still a member of the Blackburn Football Committee until his retirement from teaching in 1969, when he was made a Life Member of Blackburn Schools' Athletic Association. Altogether he gave thirty six years service to schoolboy football.

From the minutes of the first Annual Report, the Committee felt that the number of school games was not sufficient, but whenever a revision of the competitions was considered *'much difficulty is experienced due to the lack of suitable grounds.'* This was a theme that was to continue for the next thirty five years or so. Also it was felt at this time that there should be a new competition for junior schools.

Fortunately, early in the following year, 1934, the Jubilee Shield was presented to the Association by J.W.Turner Esq. to commemorate the Silver Jubilee of King George V and Queen Mary. This trophy was allocated to the junior schools - children up to scholarship age limit. Mr. J.W.Turner was a local businessman who ran 'The Little Diamond Shop' at 3 Higher Church Street, Blackburn.

This new competition fully justified itself in so far that twenty three schools took part and twenty six games were played. The first Jubilee Shield final took place at Griffin Park on Wednesday evening, 29th May 1935 and was between St.

Bartholomew's and Park Road School. The local newspaper reports described the class of football as very high with '...*the winners exhibiting very pleasing forward movements and the lads constantly making openings for each other. There was none of the wholesome rushing after the ball and the wild lunges that is too often seen among young players.*'

St. Bartholomew's were quickly four goals up through McQuirk, Harker, Haworth and Tennant, and after Park Road scored through Cowell, Tenant scored another fine goal. St. Bartholomew's won by five goals to one, and in becoming the first holders of the Jubilee Shield, St. Bartholomew's had beaten Griffin, St. Andrew's, St. Luke's and St. Peter's R.C. School.

After the game, Mr. Ben Aspinall, Chairman of the Football Committee, thanked Mr. Turner for his generosity in providing the Jubilee Shield and then asked him to hand it to the winning captain. St. Bartholomew's team was: G.Blake, E.Hargreaves, A.Holme, F.Place, C.Harker, E.Chadwick, T.Bullen, H.Haworth, C.McQuirk, H.Edmundson and T.Tennant.

The other schoolboy finals of 1935 were all played at Ewood Park. On Monday 20th May, Emmanuel beat St. Thomas' two goals to one to win the Thornton Shield and C.E. Central defeated Audley Council School by four goals to one to win the Stanworth Cup.

The finals of the Harry Boyle Cup and the Forrest Cup were played as usual on Shrove Tuesday. Blakey Moor won the Forrest Cup for the seventh time beating St. Aidan's by four goals to one, with goals from Hothersall (2), Topham and Dewhurst.

There can seldom have been a more thrilling finish than in the Harry Boyle final between St. Peter's R.C. School and St. Thomas' C.E. School. For three-quarters of the game St. Thomas' had dominated and with a three goal lead looked like running out easy winners. Then St. Peter's staged a remarkable recovery scoring three times in eight minutes through Baldwin and left winger Horner who scored twice. The game finished 3-3 and Horner was literally mobbed by his colleagues and spectators at the end.

This was also the first occasion when programmes were issued at the Ewood finals. This pleased the local reporter who stated that, '*Apart from the assistance to spectators (to whom the little fellows on the field have all looked alike), there is a wealth of interesting information.*'

This information included the fact that at least half a dozen former schoolboy players were now with League clubs. Walter Crook, the Rovers left half, had previously played for Blakey Moor and before that St. Aidan's. Others were Hacking (Manchester United) at St. Aidan's, Spink (Oldham Athletic) at St. Aidan's and then the Grammar School, Readett (Burnley) at Christ Church and then Blakey Moor, Crompton (Luton Town) at C.E.Central and Walsh (Millwall) who had previously attended St. Andrew's.

Of these Walter Crook had by far the most illustrious career, making 237 appearances for the Rovers and gaining international honours with one war-time game for England in 1939. He later coached Ajax in Holland and was manager of

Wigan Athletic and Accrington Stanley before becoming trainer-coach at Preston North End, where he remained for eighteen years.

The replay of the 1935 Harry Boyle Cup again resulted in a draw after extra-time so for the one and only time in the history of the Blackburn Schoolboys' Cup the trophy was shared. Both St. Peter's R.C. and St. Thomas' C.E. were deemed to be joint winners and both sets of players received winners medals.

In previous years winners' badges had been made at the Technical College, but during 1934 the 'cards' on which they were made had been destroyed. Later that year, the Principal of the Technical College, Mr. Wilkinson, was approached with regard to the weaving of badges once again for the Football Association. Mr. Wilkinson promised to supply badges if some scheme could be formulated whereby prizes would be offered to the students of the college for the best designs. By the end of 1934 a committee had been appointed to consider the design of the badges and it was agreed that two prizes would be given for the competition; the first prize to be one guinea (£1.05) and the second, half a guinea. The eventual winner of the prize for the best design of the badges was one Herbert Grimshaw.

The finals of the following season, 1936, produced some interesting results in that out of the five cup competition, four schools won trophies for the very first time. Mill Hill Congregational School realised an ambition of many years by carrying off the Harry Boyle Cup, their first success in any competition. They beat St. Paul's C.E. School 2-0 with goals from E.Marr and C.Todd.

Local newspaper reports say that the game was dominated by G.Stevenson, the Mill Hill centre half who on one occasion hit the opposing crossbar from a free kick inside his own half. In fact Stevenson went for an international trial match at York the following week but unfortunately did not make the England squad.

This game was followed by the final of the Forrest Cup which was won by C.E. Central who beat St. Alban's Higher Grade 4-0 with goals from Peet, Abbott, Sewell and King. C.E. Central School had been prolific winners of cup competitions for many years.

Both these games were played at Ewood Park and according to reports, *'There was a delightful little ceremony in the dressing room after the games, when the Mayoress (Mrs.W.Coupe) presented the cups to the winning captains, Stevenson and Rawcliffe; and medals to all four teams.'* Also present were Mr.G.F.Hall (Director of Education) and Mrs.Hall, Mr.D.G.Hartley (Assistant Director of Education) and Sir William Forrest (Chairman of the Education Committee).

Sir William Forrest said he never imagined his trophy would have created such interest. He paid tribute to the teachers of the town for giving their time freely in order to allow boys to play these games. Thanks were given also to the referee and linesmen and to the Rovers for allowing the use of the ground.

In the other Ewood finals of 1936 Mill Hill St. Peter's beat St. Thomas' 2-0 with goals from Metcalf to win the Thornton Shield and in the junior section of the Central Schools Competition, St. Alban's beat Blakey Moor 5-2 after extra time, with goals from Rawcliffe, Dickinson, Smith, Slater and Wearden, to win the Stanworth Cup. Both these teams won trophies for the first time.

The St.Gabriel's Team who won the Jubilee Shield in 1936. *Back row from the left*: Mr.I.Breckell (caretaker), Mr.H.Rydings (headmaster), Rev.A.Smith. *Middle*: J.Lishman, J.Ashworth, H.Jones, A.Ashworth, R.Parkinson, J.Barnes. *Front*: W.Hargreaves, A.Dewhurst, F.Dewhurst, W.Buck, W.Haresnape.

The other final to be played that year was for the Jubilee Shield and featured St. Gabriel's and St. Luke's. Mr.Hargreaves, a member of the St. Gabriel's team and now in his seventies, recalls the disappointment for the players at not playing at Ewood Park. The match was played at Roe Lee on Monday, 15th June with a 7 o'clock kick off and admission was 2d. for adults and 1d. for children. St. Gabriel's beat St. Luke's by four goals to one with Fred Dewhurst scoring a first half hat-trick and James Barnes adding another in the second half.

Captain Fred Dewhurst recalls that Mr.Whipp, who had a butcher's shop just off Whalley New Road, had promised Fred 3d. for every goal he scored and he remembers vividly feeling a wealthy young boy as he went in the shop the following day to collect his 9d. Fred was later to enter the teaching profession and will be fondly remembered by pupils at the Grammar School from the 1950s to the 1980s.

St. Gabriel's School Team who won the Jubilee Shield in 1941, once again with Mr. Breckell and Harry Rydings, the head-master.

Also in 1936, the Blackburn Association staged its first ever county game with Lancashire Schoolboys playing Yorkshire at Ewood Park. According to reports at the time, *'The game revealed a standard of football which amazed those who witnessed the game.'* Moreover, the County Association were completely satisfied with the arrangements made for the match by the Blackburn Committee.

By the following year the problem of suitable pitches was becoming more acute, with the Griffin Ground being very unreliable and often unplayable. More and more games were having to be played at Roe Lee and often schools from the Western Division were having to travel across the town. Mr. Blackburn, the Association Secretary, reminded schools that *'...tram and bus tickets to and from Roe Lee ground were available through the Education Office.'* However, things became so bad that the Jubilee Shield competition had to be temporarily discontinued and so there were no winners for 1937.

```
                    FOOTBALL SECTION.
         INCOME.          £  s. d.              EXPENDITURE.            £  s. d.
To Balance from 1935-36 ........  36  9  1   By Senior Finals—Medals ............ 12 13  0
 ,, Senior Finals—Gate ..........   £3  2 10                Match Expenses ..........  7  5  6
              Sale of Tickets ....  18 17  4   ,, Junior Finals—Medals ............   9 12  6
                                   —————                   Match Expenses ..........  7 16  6
                                    22  0  2   ,, Hire of Playing Pitch ............   0  8  0
 ,, Junior Finals—Gate ..........    5  4  6   ,, Engraving Trophies 9/-, Stationery 7/6 ...  0 16  6
              Sale of Tickets ....   9 19  2   ,, Subscription—Referees' Association ....   1  1  0
                                   —————       ,, Share General Expenses ............   2  9  1
                                    15  3  8   ,, Expenses—Secretary £1/14/1  Treasurer 2/3  1 16  4
                                                ,, Western Division Secretary's Expenses ...   0  7  7
                                                ,, Town Team—
                                                    Secretary (Grants to) .......... £10  5  3
                                                    Sundries ............................  1  1  6
                                                    Insurance .......................... 1 13  0
                                                    Twist Testimonial ................  0 10  6
                                                                                      —————
                                                                                       13 10  3
                                                ,, Balance—Secretary 10/-, Town Team Secre-
                                                    tary £3/11/2 ..........................  4  1  2
                                                ,, Balance, Bank ..........................  11 15  6
                                    £73 12 11                                         £73 12 11
```

The Statement of Accounts for the Football Section of the Blackburn Schools' Athletic Association, 1936/37.

The 1937-38 season did see the inauguration of a new competition for the St. Philip's Cup. This was to be a Charity Cup between the champions of Darwen schools and the champions of Blackburn. Sudell Road School won the new trophy beating Blakey Moor and the match, together with a preliminary match at Blackburn, provided a substantial donation to the Blackburn Royal Infirmary.

One problem in the 1930s which still remains to-day was the question of insurance for boys involved in school matches. As early as 1931 concern was expressed and by 1933 the General Secretary of the Blackburn Schools' Athletic Association had had an interview with the Director of Education to ascertain as to whether schoolchildren were insured when taking part in organised games out of school hours.

Ironically, and very sadly, there was a serious accident to a schoolboy during the 1934 season which brought the situation of insurance into sharp focus. Fred Haworth, while playing football for Accrington Road School on 1st December, was badly injured and this resulted in the amputation of a leg.

The Chairman of the Football Committee met with the Director of Education to ascertain the legal liability and also later met with doctors at the Royal Infirmary.

The Chairman had found that everything possible had been done for the boy; the leg had only been amputated after very serious consideration - in fact further delay might have endangered the boy's life.

The outcome of the accident was that the English Schools' Football Association became involved and a national appeal was made to all the Associations outside Lancashire. A fund was set up, the Fred Haworth Benevolent Fund, and a separate appeal was made to all affiliated Associations in Lancashire. The Blackburn Schools' Athletic Association opened the fund with a donation of 20 guineas. It was also suggested that there should be a benefit match played hopefully on some Saturday afternoon at Ewood. By the end of 1935 the Accident Fund had reached approximately £320.

Another consequence of this incident was that by 1937 teachers had problems with legal liability supervising organised games out of school hours. The local education authority found that the liability for accidents would be personal and that the Education Authority would not be responsible. Teachers had to be prepared by insurance or otherwise to meet claims of any alleged personal negligence.

During the 1930s there were many incidents recorded in the minutes of meetings about breaches of rules and regulations. For example in October 1934 there was a letter of protest from the Headmaster of St. Paul's School against St. Alban's and the fact that they had fielded an ineligible player. The football committee ordered the match to be replayed.

In October of the following year the committee discussed an incident in the St. Peter's R.C. versus St. Aidan's match when the players of St. Aidan's left the field without the referee's permission as a result of the actions of one of the schoolmasters present at the match. Mr. Ormerod, Headmaster of St. Aidan's, offered to withdraw his team and suggested that the result of the match should be the score when the players left the field (presumably St. Aidan's were losing at the time!). This suggestion was accepted by the committee and a letter of rebuke sent to the schoolteacher concerned.

The minutes of 28th February 1935, reported that St. Peter's R.C. School had informed the Secretary of the Football Committee that owing to sickness at his home, Bibby of St. Peter's had not put in the necessary 50% attendance to make him eligible for the Shrove Tuesday final. The Committee upheld its rules and Bibby was not allowed to play, although the rules concerning eligibility of players would be reconsidered at the next meeting.

In 1939, at the St. Bartholomew's versus St. Peter's match on Saturday, 14th January, there were complaints about the attitude of a Mr. Wignall towards the referee. The Football Committee heard that his behaviour was not sportsmanlike and that he persisted in shouting instructions to his team. The Chairman and Secretary interviewed Mr. Wignall about his action and presumably pointed out the error of his ways.

Also in 1939, the Football Committee themselves were in trouble when they received a letter from the Secretary of Blackburn Rovers Football Club. It stated that, *'The conduct of the children spectators was disgraceful at the Blackburn*

Boys' versus Manchester Boys' match and it must be understood for the future that unless plenty of stewards are in charge to exercise control, we shall not under any consideration allow the use of the ground for further schoolboy matches.'

The Football Committee drew up lists of rules concerning matches and the eligibility of players. For example, these included:

1. A teacher shall be in charge of each team. Violation of this rule will disqualify the team.

2. A list of players giving each boy's date of birth and signed by the headteacher shall be given to the referee before any match.

3. If a school wishes to rearrange a match, this can be done so long as it is agreeable to the opposing school and the Divisional Secretary and completed by 4 pm on the Thursday preceding the Saturday of the match.

At the meeting in 1938 Mr. Aspinall, the Chairman of the Football Committee, paid tribute to the memory of F.S. Horsfall, recalling his work for schoolboy football both for Blackburn and the County (Mr. Horsfall had been trainer of Parish Higher Grade who were the first winners of the Harry Boyle Cup in 1897). The members of the committee stood in silence in memory of Mr. Horsfall.

On the playing side, 1939 was a good year for the Town team, with three County players and two County trialists in the side. These included K. Sharples and A. Parkinson from C.E. Central and L. Cook and H. Williamson from Blakey Moor.

The team got to the final of the Lancashire competition, defeating Liverpool on the way, but losing to St. Helens in the final. They also won five games in the English Schools' Competition, defeating Preston, Nelson, Darwen, Crosby and

The Blackburn Town Team of 1939 featuring Leslie Cook on the extreme left of the back row.

Leslie Cook is mobbed by his school-mates at Blakey Moor School on hearing of his selection for England Schoolboys.

Sheffield away before losing to Manchester in the next round. Towards the end of the season, Leslie Cook of Blakey Moor School was awarded an international cap when he played left half for England Schoolboys against Wales at Birmingham. Altogether he won two caps and later went on to spend ten years at Ewood Park, making 84 appearances for the first team.

Membership of the Football Committee was looked upon as a privilege in those days and if teachers did not put in the required number of attendances they were replaced by other teachers who were anxious to serve the Association. This happened to two members in 1938/39; Mr.B.Aspinall and Mr.T.Powers had not attended the minimum number of meetings so they were replaced by Mr.W.Kelly and Mr.H.King. Harry King was to serve the Association for many years and will be well remembered especially by boys who went to the Grammar School over the next three decades or so.

One of the last changes brought about by the Football Committee before the outbreak of the Second World War was the reorganisation of the football competitions. This was undertaken because of the restructuring of the education system in the area which meant that all boys had to change schools at eleven years of age. It is interesting to note that there were many 11+ schools at this time. These were:- St. Joseph's R.C., St. Anne's R.C., St. Peter's R.C., St. Mary's R.C., St. Alban's Higher Grade, C.E.Central, Blakey Moor, Bangor Street, Accrington Road, Audley Seniors, St. Mary's Catholic College and the Junior Technical School. These would compete for the Harry Boyle Cup, the Forrest Cup and the Stanworth Cup.

There were also to be 26 junior schools divided into four leagues and based at four grounds, namely Roe Lee, Griffin, Intack and Audley. These would compete for the Thornton Shield and the Jubilee Shield.

However, a few short months later these plans were shelved because of the outbreak of war. It was decided that all local competitions would be run on a knock-out basis. Fortunately, the Director of Education granted permission for the use of the pitches for the purpose of holding matches on Saturday morning, '...*until such time as air raid precautions made it necessary to open up the grounds.'*

The Football Committee must have also checked with the police to see if it was in order to play schoolboy matches at this time. A letter from the Chief Constable stated, *'...that there was no objection to the playing of organised games in the Borough or to the use of referees' whistles in connection therewith.'*

However, by 1940 it was voted upon that no medals would be awarded to the finalists, although this was later amended to state that if funds were available they would be presented at the end of the season. Things became very difficult and some schools were unable to raise a team or just did not turn up for matches. All Town team games were abandoned, teachers from the Football Committee were called to military service and the general opinion was that unless additional help was forthcoming it would not be possible for the committee to carry on.

A letter to this effect was sent to all schools, asking them to send a representative to a meeting. Fortunately there was a good response which enabled the local schoolboy competitions to continue. At this time there were also a large number of

Griffin C.E.Junior School who won the Thornton Shield in 1944. *Standing from the left*: R.Walmsley, L.Aspin, R.Parkington, K.Jaques, B.Bearshaw, Braithwaite, J.White. *Sitting*: Walsh, R.Isherwood, C.Holden, N.Hargreaves, G.Rothwell.
Headmaster, Mr.Dickenson, is in the middle at the back. Because many male teachers were called into the forces, female teachers took on the role of looking after football teams during the war. At the back on the left is Miss N.Durham and on the extreme right Miss Shuttleworth, deputy head.
Roy Isherwood went on to join the Rovers and made 57 appearances for the first team over a six year period.

The St.Luke's Team. *Back row from the left*: Ken Heywood, Joe Nixon, Lindsay Wallace, Jack Leeming, Harry Pomfret. *Middle*: Mr. Tom Houlding, Clifford Woods, Alan Forrest (Capt.), Tom Russell, Derek Salkeld. *Front*: Ray Kelly, Billy Smith.

vacancies on the Central Council due to war service and it was decided that 'comforts' to the value of 7s-6d. (37p) each be sent to all the Football Committee members serving with the forces.

At the meeting in September 1939 of the Central Council it was decided to postpone the A.G.M. sine die. However, it was always the intention to resume activities when appropriate and in May 1944 the council reformed. The Football Committee were thanked for continuing to run the five competitions year by year and '...the thrill of playing on Ewood Park has been afforded to 88 boys taking part in four finals there each year.'

Two of the winning teams were Griffin C.E. Junior School, who won the Thornton Shield in 1944, and St. Luke's who won their first ever trophy, the Thornton Shield, in 1945. They beat Audley Council School by five goals to one with Smith (3), Kelly and Forrest the scorers. The players had to take clothing coupons to school so that they could have a new strip for the final. One member of the team, Lindsay Wallace, played non-league football for many years, mainly at Clitheroe, while Ray Kelly enjoyed great success as the wicketkeeper for East Lancs. Cricket Club for many seasons.

It is a tribute to the dedication and commitment of many teachers that all five major competitions were played for during these difficult and troubled times.

Score Every Time
with
TOMMY BALL'S
(Supplies) Ltd.

Retail Footwear Superstore
- Quality Brands -

* * *

HART STREET MILL
BLACKBURN
LANCASHIRE, BB1 1HW

* * *

Telephone:
(01254) 261910

Winning Team
FOR BUSINESS AND INDUSTRY

Investment funds for growing businesses

Industrial and commercial property

Management and skills training

Innovation and technology

Business advice and practical support

You'll be over the moon with our Business Support Services

LANCASHIRE ENTERPRISES

Enterprise House, 17 Ribblesdale Place,
Preston, Lancashire PR1 3NA. Tel: (01772) 203020

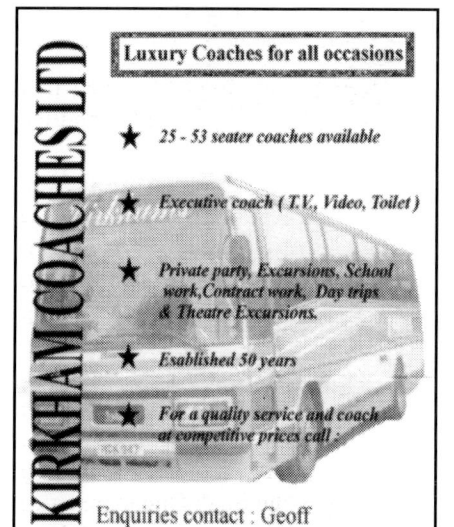

FRED KIRKHAM COACHES LTD

Luxury Coaches for all occasions

★ *25 - 53 seater coaches available*

★ *Executive coach (T.V., Video, Toilet)*

★ *Private party, Excursions, School work, Contract work, Day trips & Theatre Excursions.*

★ *Established 50 years*

★ *For a quality service and coach at competitive prices call:*

Enquiries contact : Geoff
Telephone : (01254) 232336
Fax : (01254) 388254

172 Blackburn Road, West End, Oswaldtwistle, Lancashire BB5 4NZ

WILKINSONS
SOLICITORS

Practising in Blackburn
Since 1830

Partners
John Leigh, RD*, LL.B.
Judith M. Lupton, LL.B.
David J. Hindle

1A Strawberry Bank
Preston New Road
BLACKBURN
BB2 6AS
Telephone: (01254) 51147/59191
Fax: (01254) 672914

Chapter 4
1946-1962, 'Please don't pinch the apples'

At the end of the war, things got back to normal fairly quickly. By season 1946/47 the Football Committee had again affiliated with the Lancashire Schools' F.A. and the English Schools' F.A., and the operation of school leagues and the town team had begun again.

Problems with the condition of grounds before the war had given the Football Committee the idea that every school in the Borough should have its own playing fields. Although this idea was put to one side during the war, the committee now felt that, *'this matter has now become one of national importance demanding post-war action.'*

Of more immediate concern to the Blackburn Schools' Athletic Association was the whereabouts and condition of its various trophies and it was decided to recall all trophies for examination and renovation where necessary.

In 1947, the Football Committee was rewarded in some ways for its wartime efforts when Jack Wareing of Blakey Moor and formerly of Wensley Fold School was selected for international honours. Jack gained three caps for England Schoolboys, all games played in the Victory Shield Competition. He played against Wales at Swansea, against Scotland at Goodison Park, Liverpool, and away against Northern Ireland, whose team included Harry Gregg and Jackie Blanchflower who both later played for Manchester United. Jack, who played left half and who was accompanied on these trips by Mr.Haworth, the Town Team Secretary, was the third and last Blackburn Schoolboy to achieve international honours at this age level.

Jack Robinson, also of Blakey Moor School, was selected for an international trial match during this season but failed to make the final England squad. Not surprisingly, the Blakey Moor School team were much too strong for other schools in Blackburn and won

Jack Wareing, Blackburn schoolboy who, following the international trial match at Derby on Saturday, was selected to play left half for England against Wales at Swansea on May 3.

40

ENGLISH SCHOOLS FOOTBALL ASSOCIATION
THE VICTORY SHIELD COMPETITION.
ENGLAND v SCOTLAND
AT GOODISON PARK, LIVERPOOL, 10th MAY 1947.

The England Schoolboy Team before the game against Scotland at Goodison Park, Liverpool, on the 10th May 1947. Jack Wareing is the player in the white shirt on the extreme right of the back row.

the Stanworth Cup in 1945, the Forrest Cup in 1946 and the Harry Boyle Cup in 1947.

Things were running sufficiently smoothly that by 1948 there was a new venture with the start of Town team matches for juniors. Matches against Blackpool were arranged and proved highly successful. Also in this year there was another innovation with the Association holding its first Dinner and Dance. This was to be the first of many formal Dinner and Dances organised, initially, by Ernie Rawcliffe and held in such places as Salmesbury Hall, King George's Hall and the Mecca Ballroom on St. Peter's Street.

Later they were held at the East Lancs. Cricket Club, the Polish Club and one of the last was at the De Tabley, Ribchester, in 1974. Guests at this event included the Mayor and Mayoress (Dr. and Mrs. Murray), Councillor T.Taylor M.B.E. (Chairman of the Education Committee) and Mrs. Taylor, and the oldest, most faithful and one of the founder members of the Association, Frank Littlewood. There would be one or two further Dinner and Dances before they stopped due to lack of support.

During 1948 the Football Committee gave its appreciation to two long-standing members, Mr. R.L.Senior and Mr. J.T.Riding who had both served the Association for many years and who were both retiring.

And so into the 1950s when all the secondary school competitions involving the Harry Boyle Cup seemed to be dominated by the Technical and Grammar School, Blakey Moor or St. Peter's Secondary Modern. In fact every year between 1953 and 1962, all the secondary competitions involving the Harry Boyle Cup, the Stanworth Cup and the Forrest Cup were won by these three schools. The only exceptions were Witton Park who won the Forrest Cup in 1959 and St. Mary's College who won the Harry Boyle Cup in 1962. Altogether over this ten year period the Technical and Grammar School won twelve trophies, St. Peter's ten trophies and Blakey Moor six.

Such was the domination of these schools that there was a motion put forward at one of the meetings that there should be some sort of handicapping for secondary schools or even a reorganisation of the competitions so that the smaller secondary schools might have a chance of winning something.

In season 1953/54 the Technical and Grammar School, being the champion school of the year before, represented Blackburn in the Daily Dispatch Cup. The 'Tech' went from strength to strength and eventually won the Divisional Cup by defeating Rhyddings School from Oswaldtwistle at Griffin Park. They were eventually beaten by Broughton Secondary Modern School at Salford having

St.Aidan's Junior School, winners of the Thornton Shield in 1947. Mr.T.Ormerod, the head teacher on the left of the picture, was associated with schoolboy football at St.Aidan's for nearly thirty years.

reached the last eight of the competition.

There was some dispute about this Daily Dispatch Cup, with the Football Committee generally in favour of not entering because of the difficulty in fitting in all the fixtures. However, the schools that won the right to be Blackburn's representatives were usually keen to take part so they were allowed to enter. The Football Committee insisted that this would be at no financial cost to themselves so individual schools had to pay the costs involved.

The Harry Boyle Cup was now competed for before Christmas so that the winner could go on to represent Blackburn in the New Year. Things must have been running behind schedule in 1954 when the final was arranged for the morning of 24th December at Griffin Park.

Another thing which affected secondary teams at this time was the fact that some boys could leave school at Christmas in their fourth year, dependant on their dates of birth. It must have been very frustrating for team managers and players alike if two or three decent players left and made a good team into a moderate one. For example, the Town team report of 1956/57 states that, 'once again, however, Christmas leavers proved our downfall.'

1956/57 was also the Diamond Jubilee of schoolboy football in Blackburn and in part celebration of this a County match was organised at Ewood Park. Members of the Football Committee were given various jobs; some in charge of accommodation, some in charge of reception, some looking after advertising (in buses, cinemas, shops, newspapers and hoardings), others in charge of programmes, tickets, stewarding and the after-match hospitality at Salmesbury Hall.

Tickets for the match were priced at 6d. for children in the ground, one shilling for adults, and up to two shillings and sixpence in Stand A. A profit of £138 was made on the game. Blackburn had two county players during this season. John Fletcher of St. Mary's College and Barrie Ratcliffe of the Tech. Fletcher played against Durham and Ratcliffe against Cheshire and Yorkshire. Unfortunately Barrie Ratcliffe had to have a cartilage operation during the season otherwise it was felt that he would have won international honours. However, he did go on to become a member of the Blackburn Rovers F.A. Youth Cup winning team of 1958/59 and later played fifty games for the first team at Ewood. Incidentally, Ratcliffe is one of the few footballers to be bitten in public. During a match against Manchester United at Old Trafford in October 1962, he went down in a tussle with Harry Gregg, the United keeper, who then dug his teeth into Ratcliffe's thigh before he could get up.

The 1950s were a very good time for producing future professional players who went on to great things. During the 1955/56 season Fred Pickering of St. Mary's R.C. School played twice for Lancashire Schoolboys and was later captain of the Rovers F.A. Youth Cup winning team in 1958/59. Towards the end of the 1950s John Byrom of St. Peter's C.E. Secondary Modern was making a name for himself at Schoolboy level. John was a member of the school team that won the Harry Boyle Cup in 1958 (St. Peter's also won the Clarence Walton Cup and the

A clean sweep for St.Peter's C.E.Secondary Modern School in 1950. The proud captains display the four trophies won - the Harry Boyle Cup, the Forrest Cup, the Stanworth Cup and, at the front, Gary Talbot with the Philips Cup for 1st Years. Gary went on to play professional football, mainly at Chester.

Stanworth Cup that year) and a member of the Town Team in 1959. He was later to gain England Youth International honours and give outstanding service to both Blackburn Rovers and Bolton Wanderers.

By the beginning of the 1962 season Blackburn Rovers had four ex-schoolboy players playing regularly for the first team. These were Ratcliffe, Pickering, Byrom and perhaps the greatest of them all, Bryan Douglas. 'Duggie' was by this time a seasoned international, playing in all England's World Cup games in Chile in 1962 and ending up with thirty six caps.

Bryan Douglas had attended St. Bartholomew's Junior School and had transferred to Blakey Moor towards the end of the Second World War. He played Town team football in season 1947/48, made his debut for Rovers in 1954 and went on to make 502 appearances for the first team, scoring 115 goals.

Also on the Rovers books at this time were ex-schoolboys Alan Bradshaw (Audley Juniors and Queen Elizabeth's Grammar School), a member of Rovers Youth Team in 1959, and Roy Isherwood (Griffin Juniors and St. Peter's C.E. Secondary Modern) who played fifty seven games for the first team between 1957 and 1962.

Bryan Douglas in the Blakey Moor Team which won the Forrest Cup in 1947/48. *Back row from the left*: A.Duxbury, Mr.C.Walton, headmaster, A.Cronshaw, J.Wild, R.Whalley, Mr.E.Haworth, P.Berry. *Middle*: A.Slinger, B.Douglas, R.Croft, C.Dickinson, A.Cottom. *Front*: F.Aspin, J.Leeming. Headmaster, Mr. Clarence Walton, was a keen supporter of schoolboy football. Upon his death in 1957 his wife presented the Clarence Walton Cup to the Association in his memory.

'Duggie' turns away after scoring Blackburn Schoolboys third goal in the match against Nelson Schoolboys at Ewood Park in 1947/48.

The Under-14 Blackburn Town Team of 1950/51 with the Kay Cup. *Back row from the left*: Eric Heckbotham, Joe Skehel, Ken Slater, Brian Miller, Barry Johnson, Baz. Bowman, Derek Norse. *Front*: Gary Talbot, Geoff. Higgins, Denis Barker, Ken Adcroft, Ken Greenwood, Eric Crombie, Terry Fletcher, Colin Maudsley. The following season two of this team played for Lancashire Schoolboys, Ken Adcroft and Brian Miller. Brian Miller was some ten years later to gain one full international cap and give outstanding service to Burnley as a player, manager and chief scout.

The Junior School Town Team of 1952 which defeated Blackpool away. This team features Barrie Ratcliffe, extreme right on the middle row, who was a member of the Rovers F.A. Youth Cup winning team of 1959 and who played fifty games for the first team. Also sitting on the floor on the left is Fred Pickering, captain of the Rovers Youth Team in 1959, who made 158 appearances for the Rovers first team before his transfer to Everton for £85,000 in 1964. Later in that year Fred made his full England debut, scoring a hat-trick against the United States.

The Blackburn Schools Under-14 Town Team of 1955 with the Kay Cup. Sitting on the floor are Fred Pickering and Dennis Cook who was later well-known in local non-league football. The teacher on the back row is Mr. Gregson of Blakey Moor School. The captain of the team, holding the cup, is Roy Burns of Blakey Moor, who must hold the record for goals scored in one match for Town teams. In the English Schools' Trophy competition, first round tie, Roy scored eight times in the 11-1 win over South Fylde Boys, with the other goals coming from Cook (2) and Pickering.

The 1954/55 Senior Town Team.

The 1956 Town Team.

The Blackburn Schoolboys Town Team of 1961 featuring goalkeeper Neil Ramsbottom (Audley Secondary Modern). Neil signed for Bury in 1964 and went on to play for Blackpool, Crewe Alexandra, Coventry, Sheffield Wednesday, Plymouth Argyle, Blackburn Rovers, Miami (U.S.A.), Sheffield United, Bradford City and AFC Bournemouth. The full line-up, *back row from the left*: A.Bond (referee) B.Dawson, J.Tomlinson, R.Grogan, N.Ramsbottom, T.Walsh, P.Fielding. *Front*: M.Chapman, J.Smalley, D.Adams, R.Smith, N.Reid.

1962 also saw another ex-Blackburn schoolboy making his debut for the full England team. This player actually played in the same international side as 'Duggie' making two ex-schoolboys in the same England team. This other international was Brian Miller who in 1952, along with Ken Adcroft (Technical High School) had been selected to play for Lancashire Schoolboys while attending St. Mary's College.

1959 was an outstanding year for the Town teams and for the Technical and Grammar School in particular. The Tech represented the Blackburn Association in the Lancashire Schools' F.A. Champion Schools Competition, which had replaced the Daily Dispatch Cup and which was open to the champion school in each district of Lancashire and Cheshire. The Tech beat Clitheroe Royal Grammar School 4-1 away, Burnley Wood Secondary Modern 9-3, the Bolton champions 4-2 and in the semi-final Stretford Junior Technical School 5-1 away. In the final the Tech played Southlands County Secondary Modern from Chorley over two legs, winning 4-1 away and 6-1 at Griffin Park. Scorers on the second leg were Christie (2), Penny, Kenyon, Walker and an own goal. Blackburn had first entered this competition in 1925 and the Tech were the first local school to be County Champions.

Not surprisingly, the Town team of 1959 did well in the English Schools' Shield competition. On the 3rd January, they were drawn at home to Spennymoor Boys in the 5th round. This caused a few problems for the finances of the Football Committee and the Secretary, Ken Charnley, was quoted as saying, *'it doesn't pay to go too far in this competition.'* This was because under the rules of the competition the home side must foot the bill for any expenses incurred by their visitors. As Spennymoor had to travel down on the Friday, this would mean paying for accommodation and meals as well as travelling expenses. It was estimated that the final bill could be as much as £80 and considering admission to the game was 8d. for adults and 4d. for children, the Association feared a big loss financially.

In fact the loss was £70, but the team progressed to the 6th round by winning 4-1 with goals from Bracken (2) and Christie (2). Fortunately, from a financial point of view, they were drawn against Manchester Boys in the next round. Blackburn lost 4-1 but had made excellent progress in this competition. One of the team, Michael Earrey (Tech. and Grammar) was nominated as reserve for an international trial match. The team was managed by Keith Walmsley with the help of Jack Charnock and consisted of C. White (Tech. and Grammar), S.Jackson (Tech. and Grammar), H.Heywood (Audley), C.Hobley (St. Mary's College), M.Earrey (Tech. and Grammar), P.Kenyon (Tech. and Grammar), J.Bracken (Q.E.G.S.), J.Byrom (St. Peter's), T.Christie (Tech. and Grammar), A.Gaffney (Audley), I.Parker (Q.E.G.S.), Phipps (Q.E.G.S.), Walker (Tech. and Grammar), and Morris (Q.E.G.S.)

The Harry Boyle Final of 1959 must go down as one of the most exciting games with the highest number of goals scored in the history of the competition. During 1958/59 Blakey Moor Boys School was being closed down and the 4th Year boys were being integrated into the Technical and Grammar School. The Tech therefore asked special permission to enter two teams in the Harry Boyle Cup competition - one team of boys who had attended Blakey Moor and another team of boys who had always attended the Tech. Permission was granted and one of the Tech teams reached the final where they met St. Peter's C.E. Secondary Modern.

The game was played on Saturday 14th February and the score at full-time was 5-5. At one stage in the game St. Peter's had been leading 3-0 and then later 4-1 but the Tech never gave up. In extra time the Tech scored again to win the trophy by six goals to five. Scorers for the Tech were Harrison (2), Walker (2), Biggs and Christie and for St. Peter's Cotton (2), Gould (2) and Thomas. The local reporter, Ron Kennedy, stated that, *'I always feel it's a shame someone has to lose when you've seen 90 minutes thrill packed football, moneysworth for even the most hard to please supporter.'*

Town team matches for junior schools which had begun in 1948 developed during the 1950s and by 1956/57 the Primary School Town team were playing against Blackpool, Fleetwood and Accrington. In 1959 the Junior Town team were appearing in the Luther Mercer Trophy competition which they won that year by beating Burnley, Clitheroe, Accrington and Nelson and Colne. The team, managed by Roy Mayhall of St. Luke's School, consisted of: Rowe (Longshaw), Thornley (St. Bartholomew's), Holland (Audley), Bradford (Roe Lee), Hibbert (Emmanuel), Kenyon (Emmanuel), Hughes (Intack),Tomlinson (St. Luke's), Burton (St. Thomas'), Fairhurst (Lammack), Lysons (Moss Street), Ross (St. Stephen's), Stringfellow (St. Luke's) and Kendal (St. Bartholomew's).

Another competition which began in the 1950s was the Kay Cup which was played for by under-14 town teams. Although the under-15 town team was still the important one for competitions, it was felt that boys in the third year should be formed into a Town Team in preparation for the forth year at school.

As early as 1951/52 the town team defeated Clayton home and away to become the first winners of the Kay Cup, *'a handsome trophy awarded to the Champion under-14 town team in Division 5 of Lancashire'*. The under-14 Town team won the cup again in 1961/62 which was their eighth success out of the twelve years of the competition.

Despite the success of school and Town teams there was a conflict of interests between school football and youth football during the early 1950s. After one town team game three boys asked permission to leave lunch early (it was always the custom to provide a lunch after town team games) so that they could play again in the afternoon, but the Football Committee were unhappy about the boys playing twice in one day. One parent stated that he did not want his boy to play football for the school as he had a youth trial in the afternoon.

This led to meetings between the Football Committee and representatives of the Mill Hill and District Youth Football League and letters to the Lancashire F.A. about the situation. Eventually, things were sorted out amicably with two members of the Football Committee also serving on the Youth Management Committee.

Each year, at this time, the Football Committee acknowledged the help that they received from various quarters. Invariably this would be the directors of Blackburn Rovers for the use of Ewood Park for the schoolboy finals. The Committee also made donations or gratuities each year to people and organisations who had helped them throughout the season. In 1952, for example, these were:

Donation to groundsman at Pleckgate	£3-3s-0d
Donation to groundsman at Griffin	£3-3s-0d
Donation to groundsman at Roe Lee	£2-2s-0d
Donation to groundsman at Audley	£1-11s-6d
Donation to St. John's Ambulance Association	£1-1s-0d
Donation to Blackburn and District Referees	£3-3s-0d

Although substitutes were not used in the Football League until the 1965/66 season, they were allowed as early as 1952 in Lancashire Schools' F.A. matches, but the rules stated that substitutes would only be permitted up to the 33rd minute of the game, although goalkeepers could be substituted at any time.

Blackburn Schools' Athletic Association

FOOTBALL SECTION

Rules Governing the Competitions.

1.—The laws of the game shall be those of the English Schools' Football Association, except where otherwise stated. N.B. Rule 18:—In all Matches substitutes shall be allowed to replace players who are injured during a match and are thereby rendered unable to take any further reasonable part in that match. A goalkeeper may be so replaced at any time, but other players, up to a maximum of two, may be so replaced only before half time. A substitute must appear on the field of play before half-time. A substitute shall not be allowed for any player who may be injured after the whistle has been blown for half-time.

2.—All players must wear boots.

3.—The duration of each match shall be:—

Blackburn Schoolboys' Cup Competition	70 mins.
Forrest Cup Competition	60 mins.
Stanworth Cup Competition	50 mins.
Clarence Walton Trophy Competition	50 mins.
Thornton Shield Competition	30 mins.
Jubilee Shield Competition (Knock-out)	30 mins.

4.—In Knock-out Competitions, extra time may be played in drawn games at the first meeting, subject to the agreement of the teachers in charge, but extra time must be played in the case of replayed matches.

5.—Any match may be curtailed by agreement between the teachers in charge and the referee when extraordinary circumstances occur, subject to a minimum of 75 per cent. of the time stipulated in Rule 3 being played.

6.—A list of players, giving each boy's date of birth and signed by the Head Teacher, shall be given to the General Secretary on request.

7.—Each team shall be in charge of a teacher. Violation of this rule may disqualify a team.

8.—If a school wishes to re-arrange a match, this can be done so long as it is agreeable to the opposing school and the Divisional Secretary, and completed by 4 p.m. on the Thursday preceding the Saturday of the match. (This rule does not apply to Semi-Finals and Finals).

9.—In case of any dispute, notice in writing, signed by the Head Teacher, must be given to the General Secretary within three days of the dispute arising.

ELIGIBILITY OF PLAYERS

10.—All players shall be bona fide scholars of the school for which they play. A bona fide scholar is one whose name is on the roll.

11.—In the case of a boy changing schools during the season, he shall be eligible to play under Rule 10, if he has not played for his former school in that season in the same Knock-out Competition.

12.—*Blackburn Schoolboys' Cup Competition:* No player shall be eligible who is 15 years of age or over on the first day of the Secondary Modern Schools' Autumn Term.

13.—*Forrest Cup Competition:* No player shall be eligible who is 14 years of age or over on the first day of September.

14.—*Stanworth Cup Competition:* No player shall be eligible who is 13 years of age or over on the first day of September.

15.—*Clarence Walton Trophy Competition:* No player shall be eligible who is 12 years of age or over on the first day of September.

16.—*Thornton Shield and Jubilee Shield Competitions:* No player shall be eligible if above Primary School age.

17.—For the purposes of these Competitions the first day of the Autumn Term is the day on which the Secondary Modern Schools re-open after the Midsummer Holidays.

18.—The closing date for Entries for the Competitions shall be left to the discretion of the General Secretary.

19.—The winning school shall hold the trophy for twelve months.

May, 1959.

The Roe Lee Junior School Team which won the Jubilee Shield on 8th May 1952, defeating St.Aidan's C.E. School 1-0 at Griffin Ground. As was the custom in those days, the school was granted a day's holiday to celebrate the success. The teacher on the back row is Mr. Neville Roberts, later appointed headmaster of Audley C.P. School, but who died tragically in 1959.

The Audley Junior School Team of 1951/52 with the Thornton Shield. *Back row from the left*: Robinson, Arkwright, Briggs, Cullen, Walmsley, Bradshaw. *Front*: Woodhouse, Jones, Holbeck, Atherton, Klemm, Anderton. Alan Bradshaw later played for England Grammar Schools, was a member of the Rovers Youth Team which won the F.A. Youth Cup in 1959. He had eleven first games for the Rovers. While teaching at Shadsworth School he played 294 times for Crewe Alexandra and in 1979 joined Blackburn Rovers as Youth Development Officer.

St.James' Junior School Team which defeated Mill Hill St.Peter's 3-2 to win the Jubilee Shield in 1953. *Back row from the left*: Mr.Rothwell, I.Jancowski, B.Curwen, R.Pickering, B.Dixon, Mr.Towers (head). *Middle*: S.Walker, K. McCrae, K.Pomfret, M. Glaister, R.Spencer. *Front*: T.Chatterton, A.Ashton, B.Ratcliffe, T.Barton, G.Blackburn.

Longshaw Junior School - Thornton Shield winners 1955. *Back row from the left*: W.Snape, W.Maxwell, B.Gould, P.Cottam, K.Lang, G.Readett. *Middle*: F.Bond, G.Gould, D.Pemberton, M.Drane, I.Pickup. *Front*: A.Abbott, R.Silvey, I.Smith, J.Mealor.

Cedar Street Junior School, winners of the Thornton Shield in 1958. Teachers at the back are Mr.Morgan on the left and Mr.Baldwin. *Back row from the left*: G.Robinson, P.Jackson, D.Shaw, J.Westwell, H.Baron. *Middle*: D.Douglas, D.Feldwicke, P.Taylor, M.Bibb, S.Baron. *Front*: A.Ashworth, G.Talbot.

Emmanuel Junior School Team of 1957 with the Thornton Shield. The teachers are Mr. E. Brindle on the left and Mr. H. Edmundson.

Emmanuel Junior School Team of 1959 with the Jubilee Shield, also with Mr. Brindle and Mr. Edmundson. Emmanuel were one of the most successful schools. They won the Harry Boyle Cup ten times before 1939, and have won the Thornton Shield eight times and the Jubilee Shield four times as well as other local cups.

Longshaw Junior School, winners of the Thornton Shield and the Bryan Douglas Cup in 1962. *Back row from the left*: R.Varey, R.Jose, A.Bibby. *Middle*: D.Parker, K.Erwin, S.Moore, S.Aspin. *Front*: N.Simcoe, K.Brand, K.Wareham, A.McNamee, A.Holt.

Unexpected problems arose in 1956 according to the minutes of a meeting that year and the Secretary of the Football Committee was instructed to write to all secondary schools after complaints of boys arriving too early for games on Saturday mornings and stealing apples from local gardens!

Each decade seems to bring its own tributes for teachers who had worked hard for schoolboy football over a long period of time and, on occasions, for some teachers who had passed away. The Football Committee report of 1955 states that it was with deep regret that they heard of the death of Mr.H.Wilkinson, a man who worked long and devotedly to promote schoolboy football.

In 1957 it stated that, *'Schoolboy football in Blackburn suffered a severe loss during this season by the untimely death of Mr.C.Walton, Headmaster of Blakey Moor Boys' School. Mr.Walton's service to football will long be remembered and we are now indebted to Mrs.Walton for the gift of a beautiful trophy to be named the Clarence Walton Cup and awarded to the winning 1st year secondary team.'*

Just two years later came the tragic death of the Football Committee Chairman, Mr .Neville Roberts. There was no job connected with schoolboy football that Mr. Roberts had not tackled. Schoolboy football had suffered a great and irretrievable loss. The Football Committee set up a fund for his widow and three young children, and an appeal was sent to all schools. Mr. Roberts, headmaster of Audley C.P. School, had served on at least one of the Blackburn Schools' Athletic Association Committees since 1936.

The Football Committee saw the retirement of another stalwart in 1954. To quote from the minutes, *'Time marches on and even the evergreen Mr. Littlewood has retired from the scholastic fray. Schoolboy football in Blackburn has lost a great and tireless worker for Mr. Littlewood has served on this committee since its formation (1933) and held office as Chairman, Secretary and Town Team Manager. We deplore his loss to the Association but sincerely wish him a long and happy retirement.'*

Just as immediately after the war the condition of local football pitches was a matter of great concern, so some sixteen years later things were very much the same. By 1962 the Football Committee had decided that Griffin ground had ample provision for changing and washing, and at Audley ground showers were provided for teams playing on Saturday mornings. Grounds where provision was inadequate were Pleckgate, Roe Lee and Griffin Park. Roe Lee had no provision, Griffin Park had a hand basin in one corner of an old shed and Pleckgate, where most of the secondary matches took place, had two showers and some washbasins in a pavilion well away from where most teams played. Certainly there must be thousands of schoolboy footballers who recall the wooden pavilion in one corner of Pleckgate field which was rarely used, while everyone seemed to crowd into the cold, draughty Nissen hut next to the road which had no washing facilities at all. The Football Committee once again recommended that a deputation be sent to Mr.Hartley, Director of Education, to discuss what could be done to improve the facilities.

One thing that schoolboy footballers usually remember, hopefully affectionately for the rest of their lives, is the teacher who looked after their football team. The

names of the Football Committee of 1961/62 will hopefully rekindle some memories for players around this time. The committee consisted of:
 Chairman: H.King, Q.E.G.S.
 Vice Chairman: J.K.Charnley, Mill Hill
 General Secretary: G.Armistead, Longshaw
 Minutes Secretary: L.Walsh, Witton Park
 Treasurer: J.H.Peers, St. Aidan's
 Town Team Secretary: J.Crompton, Bangor Street
 Town Team Manager: J.K.Walmsley, Tech. and Grammar
 Assistant Town Team Manager: S.Whalley, Tech. and Grammar
 Secondary Schools Secretary: M.R.Gray, Audley Secondary
 Junior Town Team Secretary: A.S.Nicholson, Moss Street
 Assistant Town Team Secretary: N.Eccleston, St. John's
 Junior Town Team Manager: R.Mayhall, St. Thomas'
 Jubilee Shield Secretary: G.Longton, Mill Hill
Other members of the committee were: H.Baldwin, St. Aidan's; C.Jones, Intack; R.Blackburn, St. Aidan's; T.Duckworth, St. Mary's College; J.Morris, St. Michael's; J.Tarbuck, St. Luke's; R.Wilkinson, Audley Secondary; C.Cronshaw, St. Luke's.

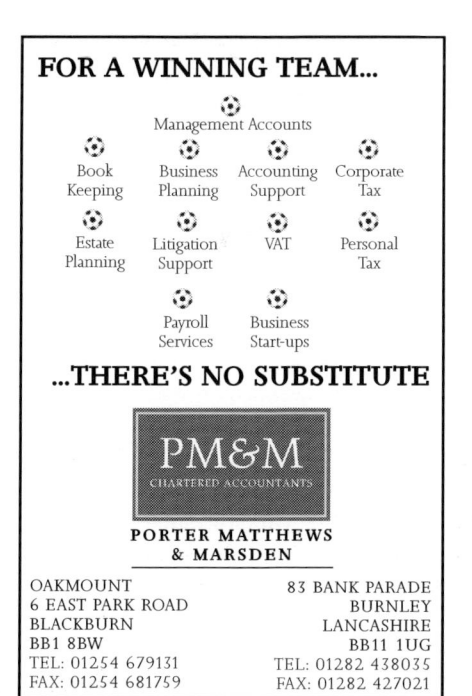

FOR A WINNING TEAM...

Management Accounts
Book Keeping | Business Planning | Accounting Support | Corporate Tax
Estate Planning | Litigation Support | VAT | Personal Tax
Payroll Services | Business Start-ups

...THERE'S NO SUBSTITUTE

PM&M
CHARTERED ACCOUNTANTS

PORTER MATTHEWS
& MARSDEN

OAKMOUNT
6 EAST PARK ROAD
BLACKBURN
BB1 8BW
TEL: 01254 679131
FAX: 01254 681759

83 BANK PARADE
BURNLEY
LANCASHIRE
BB11 1UG
TEL: 01282 438035
FAX: 01282 427021

WHITTAKERS

The One Stop Schoolwear Shop

supports

Blackburn and Darwen
Schoolboy Football

10 Ainsworth Street
Blackburn
BB1 6AD
Tel: 01254 676047

Chapter 5
1963-1979, 'The Swinging Sixties & Seventies'

At the beginning of 1963 the secondary schools in Blackburn consisted of St. Alban's, Witton Park, St. Mary's College, Queen Elizabeth's Grammar School, Accrington Road, St. Mary's Secondary, the Tech. and Grammar School, Audley Secondary, St. Peter's, Shadsworth and Bangor Street. Soon the junior schools would reorganise their competitions because of the great variation in number of pupils which attended these schools. There would be two large school leagues which would compete for the Crompton Cup and the St. Philip's Cup, and four small school leagues based at Pleckgate, Roe Lee, Griffin Ground and Griffin Park. These would compete for the Healless Cup, the Hacking Cup, the Douglas Cup and the Heatley Cup. In addition there would be competitions for the Thornton Shield and the Jubilee Shield.

The under-15 Town team did very well in 1963, reaching the final of the Lancashire Cup Competition before losing to Liverpool in the final over two legs. The team consisted of D.Stott (Q.E.G.S.), B.Pearce (St. Mary's College), R.Pickup (St. Mary's College), P.Livesey (St. Peter's), B.Sellars (St. Peter's), I.Gillibrand (Shadsworth), N.Aspin (Shadsworth), P.Jackson (Shadsworth), D.Holden (St. Mary's College), I.Kendall (Bangor Street) and A.Ross (Tech. and Grammar School).

At this time Blackburn had only ever won the Lancashire Cup on one occasion, in 1923, and had been runners-up twice in 1926 and 1939. The strength of this competition can be seen from the fact that forty two Associations entered, so to reach the semi-finals or final was quite an achievement in itself, especially against the likes of Manchester and Liverpool.

Also in 1963 Blackburn was host to a county match between Lancashire and Yorkshire. The match was at Ewood Park and the 'gate' was 1,695. After deducting costs, the net gain was £4-2s-0d. Blackburn had three representatives in the County team: I.Kendall (Bangor Street), P.Livesey (St. Peter's) and D.Holden (St. Mary's College). Livesey was later called into the England party and although he did not play he was awarded a tie and badge. Incidentally the Yorkshire delegates were provided with accommodation at three local hotels for the county game, but some of the officials refused to stay at one of them and alternative accommodation had to be hastily rearranged.

The following year Blackburn had only one representative in the County side and that was Ian Gillibrand of Shadsworth School, although John Harwood of

Q.E.G.S. was a reserve. Gillibrand played against Durham, Cheshire and Birmingham and had soon attracted the attention of League clubs. He eventually signed for Arsenal while still at school, but there was some debate as to whether he should be able to play in the Harry Boyle Cup. The question was referred to the Lancashire F.A. before the English Schools' F.A. rules were found to state that boys who had signed professional forms were not eligible to play for their schools.

The fact that Blackburn had only one representative in the County team was surprising because the Town team at this time was very strong and progressed further than any other Blackburn team in the English Trophy competition.

There were 338 Schools' Football Associations entered in the English Trophy and these were divided into 13 divisions. For the first four rounds, districts played against other teams in their division. After round four, 32 teams then went on to the next stage of the competition. Blackburn had a bye in the first round, had beaten Barrow 3-2 away, Preston 1-0 away, and Blackpool 2-0 at home to reach the fifth round where they beat Barnsley 2-1 at Griffin Park. The Town team then had a big game away to Wallsend which created a lot of local interest. The team travelled on the Friday prior to the game, seen off by Barrie Ratcliffe, John Byrom, Fred Pickering and Bryan Douglas, four ex-Blackburn Schoolboys, and stayed overnight at Whitley Bay. The groundsman at Griffin Park, Mr. Thomas

The cartoon which appeared in the Blackburn Times of Friday 31st January 1964 celebrating Blackburn Town Team's victory over Wallsend and entry into the quarter-finals of the English Trophy competition for the first time.

Blackburn Under-15 Town Team of 1964 which were the first local team to reach the Quarter-finals of the English Schools F.A. Cup competition. *Back row from the left*: P.Bradley, K.Murray, G.Kershaw, G.Hoyle, J.Wood, D.Hughes, A.Nelson, D.Taylor. *Front*: I.Neville, E.Wallace, I.Gillibrand, W.Bell, D.Geldard. Other members of the squad not pictured were J.Morris, R.Huddleston and J.Croasdale.

Ismay, who had followed the progress of the team, paid his own expenses to travel to Wallsend to see the team play. The game was played in front of an estimated crowd of 3,000 and even though the Wallsend centre forward, who apparently had a beard, scored first, Blackburn won by three goals to one and proceeded to the quarter finals.

Here they were drawn against Erdington Boys and the match was played on 22nd February 1964 at Griffin Park. Although Blackburn lost by four goals to one and were beaten by a better side, this was the first Blackburn team in the sixty year history of the English Trophy competition to reach the quarter finals. Erdington, a district of Birmingham, went on to win the Trophy.

The Mayor and Mayoress, Alderman and Mrs. F.Wilkinson, attended the match and were guests of honour at the civic reception for the Erdington party held at Witton Park School afterwards.

The Blackburn squad at this time was: J.Wood (St. Mary's Sec.), D.Taylor (St. Peter's), J.Morris (Q.E.G.S.), A.Nelson (St. Peter's), W.Bell (Shadsworth), J.Harwood (Q.E.G.S.), I.Gillibrand (Shadsworth), D.Hughes (Tech. and Grammar),

BLACKBURN SCHOOLS' ATHLETIC ASSOCIATION
FOOTBALL SECTION.

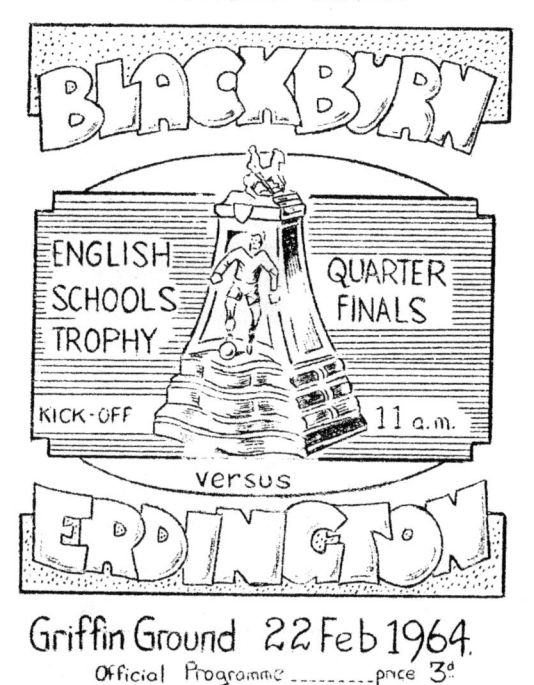

English Schools Trophy Quarter Finals — Blackburn versus Erdington — Griffin Ground 22 Feb 1964. Official Programme price 3d. Kick-off 11 a.m.

G.Hoyle (Tech. and Grammar), I.Neville (St. Peter's), R.Huddleston (Witton), E.Wallace (Q.E.G.S.), G.Kershaw (Tech. and Grammar), J.Croasdale (St. Peter's), D.Whittle (Shadsworth) and K.Murray (Witton).

Although the Rovers manager at that time, Jack Marshall, had invited all the team to sign for the Rovers on schoolboy forms, Ian Gillibrand and Ian Neville both went to Arsenal as apprentices while David Hughes joined Preston North End and later played many league games for Southport. He is the current manager of the Lancashire Schools under-19 County side.

Both the other town teams were also successful in 1964. The under-14 team beat Accrington six goals to nil in the final of the Kay Cup to win this trophy for the fifth successive year. Three of the goals were scored by outside right Stuart Metcalfe (Witton Park) who some four years later was in the senior side at Ewood and then went on to make 421 full appearances for the Rovers first team.

The junior town team also beat Clitheroe four goals to two to capture the Luther Mercer Trophy that year, with goals from Hobkirk (2), Brown and Ward.

The Chairman of the Football Committee at this time was Harry King who suffered an illness which resulted in an operation. It is recorded in the minutes that one of the members of the Football Committee had been to visit Mr.King in hospital and took with him a box of 50 Players cigarettes to HELP his convalescence. Members of the Committee subscribed to the cost of the gift, approximately 10/- (50p).

During the middle of the 1960s there was a major reorganisation of the education system as Blackburn embarked on its comprehensive policy. The old Technical and Grammar School moved out of the centre of the town up to the top of Preston New Road in 1965 and became known as Billinge Grammar School. This coincided with a very successful period for the Billinge football teams who won the Harry Boyle Cup for four years in succession, 1966 to 1969 inclusive. The 3rd year team of 1967 also won the Forrest Cup three goals to nil, with the scorers Aspin, Fowler and Charnley. Teachers at this time who had a big influence on Billinge football were 'Stan' Whalley, Rennie Nutter, Keith Walmsley and Mr.Martindale.

Everton School opened in 1966 and St. Wilfred's emerged from the amalgamation of St. Peter's Boys and St. Hilda's Girls in the same year. 1968 saw the closure of two famous old schools, as Bangor Street and Blakey Moor made way for the new Pleckgate High School.

Everton won their first trophy in 1971 when they were the first winners of the new Rigg Trophy which had been introduced for boys who now had to stay on into the 5th year. Pleckgate had to wait until 1974 when their 1st year team beat Billinge 1-0 after a replay, with a goal from Gary Ainslie, to win the Clarence Walton Cup.

The Blackburn Football Committee were again responsible for a county match when Lancashire met Birmingham and District at Ewood Park on Tuesday, 11th April 1967 with a 7 o'clock kick-off. There was a reception at Billinge Grammar School at 4.45 pm for the visiting party including a four course meal and speeches by various dignitaries. Blackburn had one representative in the county side, Phil Isherwood of Shadsworth High School who played at right-back.

Isherwood was also captain and centre-half of the Town team that season and this side proved itself to be one of the most successful ever. In the Lancashire

The successful Billinge Grammar School Team of 1967 with the Harry Boyle Cup and the Shield as Divisional Winners of the Lancashire Cup competition. No less than ten of this team were members of the successful Blackburn Town Team squad. Billinge had won the Harry Boyle Cup in 1966 and were to win again in 1968 and 1969. *Back row from the left*: Mr. Stan Whalley, D. Leaver, D. Hollinrake, B. Hodgson, K. Boland, J. Mullen, S. Bolton, P. Halleron, I. Fletcher, Mr. Keith Walmsley. *Front*: M. Lupton, A. Holt, D. Duerden, G. Stevenson, M. Hough, J. Campbell, W. Harwood, N. Purcell, J. Thompson.

Everton 5th Year Team - 1st winners of the Rigg Trophy and first team from Everton to win a cup competition. *Back row from the left*: Mr. E. Ward, Mr. R. Wilkinson, T. Solomons, P. Briggs, B. Stevenson, R. Taylor, M. Crear, S. Smith, Mr. C. Peterson. *Front*: M. Craine, J. Faries, D. Hutchinson, P. Coonan, T. Taylor, J. Holding.
Peter Briggs and John Faries both went on to teach in Blackburn schools and were both involved in schoolboy football for many years.

The first ever Cup winners from Pleckgate! The 1st Year Team with the Clarence Walton Cup which they won in the 1974. *Back row from the left*: Mr. R. Grogan, A. Mansfield, G. Widdicombe, P. Leeming, D. Richards, P. Blundell, J. Mellor (6th form). *Front*: R. Hodgson, G. Ainslie, M. Heaps, G. Talbot, D. Adams, M. Brooks, D. Crook.

Schoolboys Trophy competition, Blackburn had wins against Huyton 4-1, Middleton 4-0 after a replay, Farnworth 4-0 and Chadderton 7-1, again after a replay, to reach the final.

The final itself was a two-legged affair against a much-fancied Manchester Boys team that was studded with internationals and county players, including Tony Towers and Len Cantello, later of Manchester City and West Bromwich Albion respectively. The first leg at Griffin Park resulted in a 3-2 win for Blackburn with all the goals coming from Mullen of Billinge School. However, many thought that this was not enough with the away leg at Maine Road to come.

Against the odds, the Blackburn Boys caused a major surprise by drawing 0-0 and becoming Lancashire Schoolboy Champions. This was Blackburn's first win in this competition since 1923 and only their second ever. The team was managed by Gordon Hebden of Witton Park and was made up of: Ellis (Witton), Bolton (Billinge), Ansbro (St. Mary's College), Stevenson (Billinge), Isherwood (Shadsworth), Wells (Q.E.G.S.), Campbell (Billinge), Mullen (Billinge), Waite (Q.E.G.S.), Waddington (St. Mary's College) and Holt (Billinge). Reserves for the team were Marsden (Blakey Moor), Cameron (Shadsworth), Leaver, Hollinrake, Hough and Boland (all Billinge). Roy Wilcock of St. Wilfred's was unable to play because he had signed schoolboy forms for Blackburn Rovers.

The successful Blackburn Town Team of 1967 with the Lancashire Schools' Trophy and some of the members of the Football Committee. The Committee, *from the left*: H.King, K.Charnley, S.Whalley, T.Duckworth, K.Walmsley, F.Shuttleworth, J.Hayhurst, J.Peers, G.Longton, G.Armistead, R.Matthews. *Team, standing from the left*: S.Bolton, J.Waddington, S.Wells, R.Ellis, M.Waite, S.Ansbro. *Sitting*: A.Bradshaw (Asst. Manager), J.Campbell, J.Mullen, P.Isherwood, G.Stevenson, A.Holt, G.Hebden (Manager). *Front*: D.Leaver, S.Cameron, D.Hollinrake, W.Harwood.

From this team John Waddington joined Liverpool from school but failed to make the grade there, mainly due to a bout of glandular fever. John came to Ewood Park for a trial in 1973 and went on to play 158 games for the Rovers plus 10 as substitute.

The rest of the swinging sixties continued to flourish as far as schoolboy football was concerned. The Primary Schools' competitions were divided into large, intermediate and small schools' leagues. The large schools' league was divided into three sections, each section playing for its own trophy. After a play-off, the two winners went forward to the final of the Thornton Shield played at Ewood. The intermediate and small schools' leagues were both divided into two sections, again each playing for its own trophy. After the semi-finals, two of these teams played at Ewood for the Wightman Cup.

The Jubilee Shield was organised on a 'knock-out' basis for all schools. This meant that altogether there were ten trophies in the primary sector and several hundred boys playing football on a regular basis.

Trophies and winners for season 1969/70

Thornton Shield	St. Antony's R.C. School
Wightman Cup	St. Gabriel's C.E. School
Littlewood Trophy	St. Stephen's C.E. School
Jubilee Shield	St. Antony's R.C. School
Bob Crompton Cup	Cedar Street
Harry Healless Cup	Longshaw
Bryan Douglas Cup	St. Aidan's C.E. School
St. Philips Cup	St. James' C.E. School
Hacking Trophy	St. Bartholomew's C.E. School
Mildred Heatley Trophy	St. Gabriel's C.E. School

It could be argued that the late 1950s and '60s were the heyday of schoolboy football in Blackburn. Although right from the beginning football had developed and progressed with the number of cup and league competitions increasing for both juniors and seniors, things were really flourishing at this time with many individual schools as well as the Town teams being very successful.

This success was reflected not only in the fact that there were a number of schoolboys who made the grade in the professional game around this time. As well as those mentioned in the previous chapter who were playing for Rovers, there were players like David Helliwell (Rovers), Stuart Metcalfe (Rovers), David Hughes (Preston), Neil Ramsbottom (Bury), John Waddington (Liverpool), Neil Wilkinson (Rovers) and John Kenyon (Rovers) signing for professional clubs.

This was also still the time for teachers when membership of the Football Committee was something to aim for and by no means automatic. There were

Witton Park School who had a good season in 1966/67. Their 1st Year team won the Clarence Walton Cup and their 2nd Year's the Stanworth Cup.

The 1st Year team, *back row from the left*: J.Pomfret, J.Tattersall, M.Grunshaw, A.Wade, T.Eddleston, A.Procter, Mr.L.Walsh, M.Stanley, R.Ainsworth. *Front*: J.Dugdale, D.Houghton, N.Wilkinson, P.Baulcombe, M.Brunt. The captain of this team, Neil Wilkinson, later turned professional with the Rovers and played some 34 games for the 1st Team, plus 4 as substitute.

The 2nd Year team, *back row from the left*: J.Bolton, S.Hoole, R.Nixon, D.Zarac, J.Baron, R.Haydock, N.Wilkinson, N.Clare, Mr.G.Hebden. *Front*: L.Mason, S.Casson, D.Huzal, J.Kenyon, A.Greenwood, I.Hargreaves, P.Guppy. The captain of this team, John Kenyon, made 32 appearances for the Rovers 1st Team, plus 14 as substitute.

Roe Lee Junior School Team of 1965, winners of both the Jock Wightman Trophy and the Jack Hacking League Cup. Back row from the left: J.Dawkins, M.Haworth, P.Gleave, G.Slater, A.Procter, P.Caffrey. Front: R.Fallon, P.McGuire, G.Easton, D.Brooks, J.Fallon. Inset: E.Wilkinson. Roe Lee's record for the season was: played 25, won 21, drawn 2, lost 2, goals for 127, goals against 23.

St.Mary's 1st Year Team which won the Clarence Walton Cup in 1969 at Ewood Park. *Back row from the left*: M.Redman, M.Higgins, S.Saunders, M.Boobiet, B.Boothman, D.Mooney. *Front*: D.Higgins, M.Hohol, P.Killian, P.Sosnowski, S.Mercer, P.Morley. Mick Higgins was to reach the final trial for the England Under-15 team in 1971/72. Dave Mooney has taught in Blackburn for many years and has served on the Football Committee for most of that time.

St.Alban's Primary School who had a very successful season in 1967/68, winning the Thornton Shield, the Bob Crompton Cup and the Catholic Schools Shield. *Back row from the left*: Mr.Kenyon (sportsmaster), Fr.Charnock, Mr.H.Mercer. *Middle*: A.Cotteral, S.O'Donoghue, M.Douglas, P.Wilkinson, M.Hohol, K.Phillipson, B.Lester. *Front*: P.Turner, P.Agnew, S.Howson, S.Croak, J.Walsh.

always more people seeking to join than were needed and the dedication of members can be seen from the minutes of a meeting held shortly before the Harry Boyle Final at Ewood Park on Saturday, 13th March 1968. The Committee stressed, '*...that it was the DUTY of all members of the Committee to be present on the finals day at Ewood unless a sound and valid excuse was presented. The Chief Steward would be responsible for allocation of duties and all concerned should report at 9.30 am on that day.*'

In season 1969/70, due to the increased size of the Football Committee and the enthusiasm of several of the younger teachers, a Primary Schools Town team was re-formed, playing a couple of friendly matches. The following season the Primary Town team entered the Luther Mercer competition and, in 1972, won the trophy for the first time since 1964. The competition was played on a league basis and won by an outstanding team, with Blackburn scoring 31 goals and conceding only 3. The team was: J.Haydock (St. Antony's), M.Caton (St. Mary's), C.Ashcroft, B.Battersby, M.Haworth, M.McManus (all St. Peter's), G.Fowler (Roe Lee), P.Smith, N.Vernon (Longshaw), S.Caine, B.Moran, N.Hodgkinson, D.Howson (all St. Alban's), J.Berry (Wensley Fold), M.Dearden (St. Stephens), N.Clayton (Lammack) and A.Mason (St. James').

The outstanding secondary school of this season was undoubtedly St. Mary's College who won four out of the five cup finals. Their best player at under-15 level, Mick Higgins, was a regular in the County side and only just missed out on an international cap, reaching the last eighteen from which the England team was chosen.

The previous season the Football Committee had said farewell to two of its hard working and long serving members. Mr.J.Peers, who was a former treasurer of the Association, and Mr.G.Armistead who was retiring from the Committee after thirty years service.

In September 1970 a party of 22 senior boys and 5 teachers, led by Ken Charnley and Gordon Hebden, spent an enjoyable weekend in Peronne, Blackburn's French twin town. This trip was sponsored by Blackburn Corporation who were keen to establish links with Peronne and also with Altena, Blackburn's German twin town. The boys took part in an athletics and football competition at Peronne's new Athletic Stadium. The following year a similar trip was organised to Altena where there was a triangular competition between the host town, Peronne and Blackburn in athletics and football. Finally in 1972 Blackburn played host and Witton Park was used for the competitions.

Ken Furphy, the Rovers Manager, hands over the Kay Cup to the Blackburn Under-14 Town Team in 1972. This was Blackburn's third win in succession and they had at this time won the Kay Cup 16 times in 22 competitions. *Standing from the left*: Ingham (Pleckgate), Lucas (Pleckgate), Huddleston (Witton Park), Gallagher (St.Edmund Arrowsmith), Fillingham (Witton Park), Flitcroft (St.Wilfred's), O'Donnell (St.Edmund Arrowsmith), Szpunar (St.Mary's College), Hunt, Brun (St.Mary's College). *Front*: Fairclough (St.Mary's College), Taylor (St.Edmund Arrowsmith), Smith (Everton), Lester (St.Mary's College).

Another event which began at the beginning of the 1970s was the penalty competition held at half-time during the Rovers home games. The idea for this came from Arthur Fryars, a director of Blackburn Rovers, and was quickly taken up by the Blackburn Schools' Football Committee. A trophy was provided by the Rovers and it was decided that the competition would be for boys at under-15 level. Teams would consist of 5 penalty takers and one goalkeeper. Each player would take one penalty at the Darwen End and then walk down the pitch and take another penalty at the Blackburn End. Tommy Duckworth from St. Mary's College was the teacher who organised and was responsible for each competition.

This event continued successfully for many years although it was modified later when the Rovers did not want the goalmouths used. Portable goals were put up along the touchline at the Enclosure side of the ground. Henry Marcinkiewicz from Everton School took on the running of the competition on the retirement of Tommy Duckworth.

In 1988 an extra penalty competition for under-13 boys was set up and won by Darwen Vale, but the under-15 event was abandoned in the early stages when the Rovers banned all use of the ground by outside bodies owing to problems with the pitch. Shortly afterwards the penalty competitions came to an end as the Rovers continued trying to solve their problems with the pitch.

In 1973 the Blackburn teachers formed their own football team which entered and won the local Orphanage Cup competition at the first attempt. The final was at Ewood Park against Scapa Porritt and gave an opportunity for many local schoolchildren to shout at their teachers instead of the other way round. The teachers' team featured many who were involved with local schoolboy football at that time including Gordon Hebden, Alan Cameron, Mark Brownridge, Rick Grogan, Roger Masters, Phil Sumner, Clive Peterson, John Waddington and Chris Thayne.

Also in this year there were several meetings concerning the proposed amalgamation between Blackburn and Darwen schools. In April 1974 the Blackburn and Darwen Schools Sports' Association came into being without too many problems. This meant that the Darwen Secondary schools (Darwen Vale, Moorland and St. Thomas Aquinas) joined the Blackburn competitions and players from these schools were now eligible for the new Blackburn and Darwen Town team. Junior schools within Darwen decided to remain separate from Blackburn and to continue with their own competitions.

Another feature of local government reorganisation was that Lancashire no longer contained the likes of Bolton, Manchester, Wigan and Liverpool. They could no longer play in the Lancashire Cup competition and in fact from the 42 Associations that entered the old Lancashire competition, there were now only 11 in the 'new' Lancashire.

Probably the best thing that came out of a merging of Blackburn and Darwen, certainly from the Blackburn point of view, was the fact that a young teacher from Darwen Vale, Mike Hodkinson, became involved with the new Association. 'Hodge', as he is known to all, was the driving force behind schoolboy football in the area and was Secretary of the Blackburn and Darwen Football Committee for seventeen years. During this time he was also Chairman of the Lancashire Schools' Football Association and a selector for the County team. 'Hodge' only stood down as Secretary because he was elected to the council of the English Schools' F.A. and could no longer serve at local level.

The Darwen schools had within its ranks another very well respected administrator in schoolboy football. Bill Alder came to Darwen as a headteacher in the early 1960s, served as Secretary to the Lancashire Schools' F.A. and was elected to the English Council in 1965. Bill reached the highest office when he became Chairman of the English Schools' F.A. in 1973/74 and although he retired from teaching in 1977 his opinions and advice were sought by many of the younger generation of teachers for many years after this. A special trophy was given in his honour and each year under-15 Town teams in the North-West play for the Alder Cup - the second most important competition after the English Trophy.

The Chairman of the Blackburn Football Committee at the time of amalgamation was John Duckworth, a teacher at St. Stephen's and later headmaster of St. Silas'. John had been Secretary of the football section for four years prior to becoming Chairman in 1973/74, a position in which he continued for many years. He became President of the Blackburn and Darwen Schools' Sports Association in 1978/79 and was still involved in running schoolboy football at junior level up to the early 1990s.

During the first season of reorganisation, 1974/75, Blackburn and Darwen had a very strong side, bolstered by four players from the Darwen schools. Ably captained by Mick Duxbury (St. Mary's College), this team became Lancashire Champions by defeating Blackpool over two legs. They drew 1-1 away at Bloomfield Road and won 3-1 at Griffin Park with goals by Betts and Duxbury (2). Mick Duxbury went on to enjoy great success at Manchester United and was the last ex-Blackburn schoolboy to gain full international honours.

While the secondary Town team did very well, there were problems in the junior sector as the new Association was involved in negotiations with the new County Education Authority over teachers' car insurance. One teachers' union, the N.U.T., recommended that teachers did not use their cars for the transportation of children and consequently the primary school leagues were suspended until the whole insurance position was clarified.

Also at this time the condition of pitches left much to be desired and the standard of maintenance of playing fields was deteriorating. It is quite amazing that these two themes - insurance and the condition of pitches - continue to crop up right from the beginnings of the Football Association in 1933.

1975 saw the deaths of two ex-members of the Association who had devoted many years to schoolboy sport. Harry Mercer, whose great interest was football, served on both the football and athletics committees, and George Armistead, who had only retired four years previously but who had served the Association for most of his teaching life, inspiring others by his enthusiasm and high standards.

The Blackburn and Darwen Schoolboys Squad that won the Lancashire County Cup competition in May 1975, defeating Blackpool in the final over two legs. The captain, Michael Duxbury (holding the ball) signed for Manchester United and later won an F.A. Cup Winner's Medal and was the last Blackburn Schoolboy to win an international cap. Steve Mullen, left on the back row, later went on to play professionally at Bury.
Back row from the left: S.Mullen (St.Thomas Aquinas), D.Wilkshire (Moorland), G.Hecker (Moorland), P.Betts (St.Mary's College), E.Green (Pleckgate), I.Walsh (Witton), T.Grunshaw (St.Edmund Arrowsmith), M.Caton (John Rigby), D.Clarke (Witton). *Front*: T.Conroy (Everton), B.Rogers (Witton), C.Rigby (Darwen Vale), M.Duxbury (St.Mary's College), P.Beardsworth (St.Mary's College), J.Hamilton (St.Edmund Arrowsmith), M.Fraser (St.Mary's College).

    Retiring at this time were Clarence Fairhurst, another long-serving member and former President of the Association, and Jim Hayhurst who continued for many years to help with and support the Town teams and was eventually made a life member of the Lancashire Schools' F.A. in 1985.

    In the later years of the 1970s there were many notable highlights for the Football Committee to reflect upon. In 1976 the English Schools' F.A. allowed the Blackburn and Darwen Association to stage the England Schools' under-18 versus the Scotland Schools' under-18 game at Ewood Park. This was the Association's first international and it was a tremendous success.

    Under the chairmanship of John Duckworth, Secretary Mike Hodkinson and Treasurer Gordon Walker of Shadsworth Junior School, the committee managed to pull in a gate of 8,000, which was more than several of the Rovers Division 2 games that season.

The Saxon Hotel (now the Moat House) was the base for both sides and the pre-match reception was also staged there. St. Mary's College was used for training and the result of the game, a 1-1 draw, seemed almost irrelevant compared to the number of compliments that the Association received on working so hard to produce such a splendid occasion.

For the next three seasons, Blackburn and Darwen had three international players representing the Association. In 1977, J.Dootson, a pupil at Darwen Vale School, gained an under-18 cap when he went on as substitute in the away game against Scotland. The following year Eddie Green of Pleckgate School, formerly of Lammack School and a member of the successful Town team of 1975, was chosen to play in goal for England at under-18 level against Wales and Scotland. Finally in 1979 Andy Morley of St. Mary's College played for the England under-18 side also against Wales and Scotland.

During this season the under-14 Town team featured a young Mark Patterson of Darwen Vale School. Mark played for the County Schoolboys and signed as an apprentice for the Rovers on leaving school. He went on to play 98 first team games at Ewood plus 17 as substitute, including the Full Members Cup winning team of 1987. Mark has also given very good service to Bury, Preston North End, Bolton Wanderers and Sheffield United.

The captain of St.Mary's College 5th Year Team, Danny Keough, with the Rigg Trophy in 1979. Danny was one of the most talented schoolboy footballers of his era and signed forms for Manchester United on leaving school. This team in the previous season had been champion school of Lancashire at Under-15 level. *Back row from the left*: P.Waine, N.Brakespeare, M.Clements, A.Connolley, P.Murray, D.Sharples. *Front*: M.Wilson, D.Gilrane, I.Singleton, P.Belshaw, P.Loughney, P.Leaver.

Captain of St.Wilfrid's 4th Year Team, Neil Hanson, holds up the Harry Boyle Cup. St.Wilfred's won the trophy in 1979. *Back row from the left*: I.Procter, M.Meadows, N.Clemson, S.Heighway, I.Morgan, A.Hunt. *Front*: C.Eastham, S.Anderson, K.Barker, R.Bradford, J.Kelly, H.Clayton.

1978/79 marked the 75th Anniversary of the English Schools' F.A. and to celebrate the occasion they organised a Mini World Cup Tournament in the North-West. Blackburn were asked to host the Northern Ireland under-15 side and although they were regarded as underdogs, the Irish actually won the competition. Included in their team was Norman Whiteside, who only three years later was playing in the proper World Cup in Spain, and also Alan McDonald, who has played at Queen's Park Rangers for many seasons.

To show their appreciation of their stay in the area, the Irish Schools' F.A. donated a trophy to the Blackburn and Darwen Football Committee which is used for an annual 5-a-side competition at secondary level.

Schoolboy football was still flourishing by the end of the 1970s although many of the secondary schools mentioned at the beginning of this chapter had disappeared, moved or changed their name. The new secondary schools involved in football were: Pleckgate, Everton, Billinge, St. Edmund Arrowsmith, St. John Rigby, Shadsworth, Witton Park, Queen Elizabeth's Grammar School, Darwen Vale, Moorland, St. Thomas Aquinas, St. Mary's College, St. Wilfred's and Notre Dame.

One satisfying outcome of these changes was that no one secondary school completely dominated the competitions and cups were shared around. St. Mary's College, under the leadership of Tommy Duckworth, were always a force to be reckoned with, but all the secondary schools enjoyed a fair measure of success.

Chapter 6
1980-1997, 'Parent Power and into the Future'

In February 1980 the Football Association was saddened by the death of Harry King - a Life Member of the Sports Association and until his retirement from teaching, a stalwart of schools' football. Harry had joined the Football Committee in 1939 and had served schoolboy football for some thirty five years.

It is ironic that the dedication and commitment shown by Harry King and many others throughout the history of schoolboy football in Blackburn was found to be on the decline from the early 1980s. Fortunately this did not apply to all teachers, but certainly things began to change around this time. Whereas there had always been a surplus of teachers to serve on the Football Committee, gradually the goodwill that had been shown for many years towards voluntary, extra-curricular activities began to disappear.

The reasons for this were many and complex, but are basically tied up with changes in teachers' conditions of service, the introduction of directed time and later the demands of the National Curriculum. The outcome was that the focus of the profession was now very much in the classroom; in secondary schools, teachers from other subject areas who had helped the P.E.Department by running school teams now found this very difficult, while in junior schools, extra-curricular activities could not be given the priority of previous years.

The report of the Blackburn Schools' F.A. in 1982/83 expressed concern at the decline in active membership of the committee and some twelve months later described the decline in membership as a serious situation. The running of schools football was falling on the shoulders of a few loyal members, whose goodwill was now being stretched to the limit.

By 1985 the situation was made even worse when the two main teacher unions told their members to stop taking part in extra-curricular activities. The Football Committee had not wanted to stop playing football, but were now left with no option and so all activities were suspended for the 1985/86 season. On its resumption the following year it was decided to split the Football Association into two separate bodies - a Primary and a Secondary Association.

Despite all these 'off the field' troubles, the football in schools continued to do extremely well. The 1980/81 season was described as probably one of the busiest and most successful that the Association has experienced both on and off the field.

The Blackburn and Darwen Under-15 Town team equalled the record of the

1964 Blackburn side by reaching the last eight of the English Trophy Competition. They won 3-1 at Bury, beat Bootle away, thrashed Coventry 4-1 at Ewood Park, crushed Blackpool 4-0 and beat Sheffield 2-1 away at Hillsborough. This last victory has been described as possibly the finest victory in the history of the Town team.

Two coaches made their way to Hillsborough but unfortunately one of the coaches, full of supporters, missed the M1 turn off from the M62 and the driver only realised his mistake when he was on the outskirts of Hull! The coach and supporters arrived at the game immediately after half-time and their vocal support lifted the side. Goals by Peter McCrae and Anthony Haworth gave the Blackburn and Darwen side a victory over Sheffield who had, at the time, an exceptional record in the English Trophy competition.

The game itself was full of incidents. Mark Brennan, usually so composed, missed a penalty, the Sheffield centre-half was carried off with a broken leg and, amazingly at this level, two players were sent off. The Sheffield right-back was dismissed for consistently taking throw-ins from the wrong place and Mohammed Ilyas, a right-winger from Billinge, followed him down the tunnel for a late tackle.

In the quarter-final the local lads had a home tie at Ewood against South London. Shortly before this game Mark Brennan, one of the most talented players from this Association over the last 25 years, heard that he had narrowly failed to secure selection for the England side. This was a real body blow for the player and he completely lost form for a few weeks. Unfortunately against South London the performance of the rest of the team was equally disappointing and it is fair to say that their 3-0 defeat was a fair reflection of the play.

Blackburn and Darwen Under-15 Town Team which reached the final of the Lancashire Cup and the last eight of the English Schools' F.A. Trophy in 1980/81. *Back row from the left*: P.Briggs (manager), R.Morley, M.Young, G.McCrae, M.Houldsworth, S.Eagleton, P.Dunlop, D.Riley, G.Heap, P.McCrae, A.Haworth, M.Brennan, A.Cameron (Manager). *Front*: M.Ilyas, C.Watkins, S.Bolton, M.Bennett, W.Slater, C.Smith, D.Burnside.

Mark Brennan enjoyed a long career in the professional game, playing at Ipswich, Middlesborough, Manchester City and Oldham.

Winners of the Harry Boyle Cup in 1981 were Moorland School from Darwen. Captain, Mark Bennett, with the Trophy was also a member of the highly successful Town Team of that year. *From left to right*: R.Catterall, G.Welsh, R.Baron, S.Roberts, D.Dawson, P.Hawthornthwaite, Hawthornthwaite, D.Reilly, D.Knowles, M.Walkden, M.Bradshaw, C.Nicholson, N.Balshaw. Teacher, Mr.P.Cook, is at the back.

However, this very talented side went on to reach three finals. They won at Leeds to win the Northern Merit Trophy, defeated Bolton in the final of the Alder Cup and lost narrowly to Blackpool in the Lancashire final.

The centre-back in this team was Michael Young, an under-age boy from the small St. Thomas Aquinas School in Darwen. Michael was a big lad for his age and played for Lancashire Schoolboys for two consecutive seasons, representing the North-West team and in his final game for the Blackburn and Darwen team against Leeds in May 1982 he actually made his 100th Town team appearance - a remarkable record which, I suspect, will never be repeated. The managers of this outstanding Town team were Alan Cameron of Witton Park School and Peter Briggs of Pleckgate School.

The primary schools Town team, under the direction of Peter Hopwood, Phil Gardner and George Crowther, had a successful season, winning the Luther Mercer Shield and just losing in the final of the Lancashire Primary Schools' Trophy. Altogether this team played some 17 games, winning 10, drawing 4 and losing 3. The squad consisted of M.Harrison, R.Buckley, M.Gaskell (all Meadowhead School), L.Clarke, J.Whittle, S.Howard (all St. Aidan's School), C.Robinson, M.Hammond, J.Melia (all St. Peter's Junior School), L.Carus (St. Francis), J.Brown (Griffin Park), P.Duffel (Holy Souls), C.Westwood and L.Spencer (both Feniscowles Junior School).

Everton School Under-15s who won the Harry Boyle Cup in 1982.
Back: C.Flynn, T.Craig, A.Hatch, S.Smith, A.Taylor, M.Pledger, A.Khan, Mr. H. Marcinkiewicz.
Front: B.Derbyshire, L.Chadwick, B. Hartland, D.Chadwick, M. Dudhwala, C.Riley, D. McKillop.

Blackburn Primary Town Team of 1981/82. They played 15 games, winning 4, drawing 3 and losing 8. *Back*: C.Nelson, C.Blow, N.Farrell, J.Mercer, S.Sutcliffe, J.Guest, M.James, M.Finley.
Front: P.Mercer, R.Morris, C.Farnworth, A.Taylor, H.Greaves, M.Saurin.

By the 1982/83 season the Football Committee had arranged a sponsorship deal with Crown Paints from Darwen and this proved very beneficial to schoolboy football in the area. As well as coaching courses at both primary and secondary level, the sponsorship of Crown Paints enabled the Association to initiate an indoor primary five-a-side competition and the new trophy became known as the Jim Hayhurst Cup. The first winners were Roe Lee School.

The Football Association, with the assistance of Crown Paints, were also able to hold a very successful Presentation Dinner with guest Phil Neal of Liverpool and England, and Gordon Taylor from the Professional Footballers' Association. This was to be the first of many such Presentation Evenings and other guests over the years included Bob Paisley, the Liverpool manager, and International players Steve Coppell, Sammy Lee, Mark Lawrenson and Jim Beglin.

The six year partnership between the Football Committee and Crown Paints finally came to an end in 1988 and the Association was very grateful for the financial support it received over that period.

There were many other innovations during the 1980s. For example Sid Green of the St. Helens Association and the North-West representative on the English

Schools' F.A. Council instigated a North-West schoolboy team. Although they only played one game a season against the Midlands, it was a great honour to be selected. The following boys enhanced the status of the Blackburn and Darwen Association by playing in these fixtures:

1980	Mark Brennan	St. Mary's College
1981	Michael Young	St. Thomas Aquinas
1982	Neil Watson	Q.E.G.S.
1983	Andrew Dickinson	Pleckgate H.S.
1989	Lee Moss	Darwen Vale H.S.
1990	Daniel Leeming	Q.E.G.S.
1991	Karl Gaston	Darwen Vale H.S.
	Matthew Woods	Our Lady and St. John H.S.
1992	Ian Duerden	St. Wilfred's H.S.
1993	Christopher Sutton	Witton Park H.S.

It was in 1984 that Mrs.Hoole of Blackburn approached the Association and asked if she could present a trophy in memory of her late husband who was such a football fanatic. It was decided to present the J.T.Hoole Trophy each season to the under-15 Town team player who brought honour to the Association and set a good example both on and off the field.

During their six year sponsorship by Crown Paints, the Blackburn and Darwen Association had a presentation evening at the end of each season. Here, in 1987, the trophies for both juniors and seniors are presented by Jim Beglin, the Liverpool player. The captain of Pleckgate's 4th Year Team, John Coward, receives the Harry Boyle Cup from Jim Beglin.

Winners to date are:

1985	Eric Fiocca	Notre Dame H.S.
1986	Not Awarded	
1987	Tim Haworth	Q.E.G.S.
1988	Shaun McHugh	St. Wilfred's H.S.
1989	Ian McGarry	St. Bedes
1990	Gary Gaston	Darwen Vale H.S.
1991	Daniel Leeming	Q.E.G.S.
1992	Karl Gaston	Darwen Vale H.S.
1993	Daniel McNally	Q.E.G.S.
1994	Michael Krupa	St. Bedes (shared)
	Christopher Sutton	Witton Park H.S. (shared)
1995	Neil Zarac	St. Bedes
1996	Shaun Berry	Queen's Park H.S.

Town teams continued to do well throughout the 1980s. The under-15 team of 1983/84 after an indifferent start to the season, came good towards the end of the season reaching the final of the Lancashire competition. Here they met the strong and much fancied Blackpool side at Deepdale. Despite conceding an early goal, the local lads fought back to equalise and took the game into extra time. With no further goals, the Lancashire Trophy was shared for the first time in the long history of the competition. It was an achievement that seemed beyond the Blackburn and

Notre Dame High School Under-16 Team with the Cup for winning the 5th Year league competition in 1983. *Back row from the left*: B.Mooney, C.Duckworth, J.McAuley, R.Dobbin, F.Odudu, M.Johnson, P.Wiggans. *Front*: S.Gannon, N.Smith, J.Bellanca, G.White, M.Healey.

Blackburn and Darwen Under-14 Town Team at Old Trafford in 1987 for the final of the Granada Cup which was televised on I.T.V. *Back row from the left*: N.Gorton, P.Crompton, R.Procter, C.Riley, D.Riley, S.Wiggins, N.Dunleavy, J.Beattie, S.McHugh. *Front*: G.Taylor, Haworth, C.Schofield, J.Smith, C.Cameron, J.Taylor, G.Cordingley, P.Baah. Peter Baah joined the Rovers as an apprentice and made one first team appearance.

Darwen team at one stage of the season. The managers of this side were again Alan Cameron and Peter Briggs. Incidentally, Alan's three sons, Alastair, Chris and Jamie, who all attended Pleckgate School, also all played for the Town team and all played in the Lancashire under-19 side.

Another innovation, again the brainchild of Sid Green, was the start of the Granada Trophy. The I.T.V. company of that name showed interest in filming schoolboy football in 1987 and they were persuaded to sponsor an under-14 inter-Association competition throughout the Granada area with the final on a League ground. This competition ran for five seasons with money from Granada, but only for three seasons as a televised event.

During this time the Blackburn and Darwen sides excelled themselves against the other big North-West associations and reached three finals. The under-14 team of 1987 was not an outstanding side but they hit a purple patch towards the end of the season and reached the final playing Sefton at Old Trafford. Although they lost 3-0 they had the satisfaction of playing at Manchester United's ground and of the game being televised on Granada.

The following year another average Blackburn and Darwen under-14 team again played well above themselves to reach the final against Salford Boys at Anfield. The Blackburn and Darwen boys played marvellously but finally succumbed 3-2 in extra time when the Salford player Ryan Wilson scored the winner following a run from his own penalty area. The managers of the Town team, Gary Strickleton from St. Bede's H.S. and John Faries of Daisyfield Junior School were interviewed

The Intack Team who won the Jubilee Shield in 1981 at Ewood Park. *Back*: S.Bagdid, P.Talbot, P. McRobin, I.Williams, R.Kennedy, C.Barral, N.Duckworth. *Front*: M.Saurin, F.Brown, M.Coar, R.Lewis, C.Wynne, S.White, M.Law.

Sacred Heart R.C. Junior School with some of their trophies from season 1984/85. *Back*: J. Higginson, A.Neild, M.Robinson, T.Mitchell, K.Gill, J.Robinson, M.Newell. *Front*: J. McGonagle, J.Fahey, P.Bolton, D.Talbot, S.Grunshaw. Captain J.P.Booth is at the front.

on television, and they both sang the praises of young Wilson. Later Mrs.Wilson divorced Mr.Wilson, married a Mr.Giggs, Ryan changed his name and the rest is history.

Some three years later when the competition was unsponsored and the Greater Manchester and Merseyside Associations had pulled out, the Blackburn and Darwen team hammered Allendale from West Cumbria 7-0 in the final at Griffin Park.

The under-15 Town team of 1989/90 was almost an outstanding side, it contained three county players in Lee Moss, Warren Peake and Steven Haworth. It produced many good performances but never actually won anything. Striker Gary Gaston achieved a notable feat on 17th February 1990 when he scored seven goals in an 11-2 victory over Pendle.

In the English Trophy competition the team had beaten Trafford 2-1 away, Bolton 3-2 and then met Walsall at Pleasington after the original game at Ewood had to be postponed. This resulted in a goalless draw even though Blackburn and Darwen had dominated most of the game. The replay was in Walsall on 30th November 1989. This game should have been remembered as an exciting encounter with the

Blackburn and Darwen boys just losing by 2 goals to one. But events on the return journey made it a nightmare.

At 10.00 pm, about one kilometre north of the Keele Services on the M6, a blanket of fog suddenly descended and hundreds of vehicles piled into each other and two people lost their lives. The coach carrying the team, parents and supporters ran into the back of a container lorry but fortunately no-one was injured. The emergency services could not reach the injured because vehicles were strewn all over the carriageway and hard shoulder. After the passengers on the coach were taken to safety, manager Alan Cameron used his first aid skills on the many injured people and secretary Mike Hodkinson spent thirty minutes directing traffic onto the other carriageway, away from the body of a lorry driver who had been catapulted over the central reservation.

The coach party had left Walsall totally dispirited following their defeat, but by the time that they reached Blackburn at 3.00 am the following morning there was only a feeling of relief that everybody had returned safely.

The Primary Schools' Town teams were still going strong throughout most of the 1980s under a series of managers including Pete Hopwood, Phil Gardner, George Crowther, Graham Barnes, John Hacking, Steve Nicholson and Paul Gavin. 1985 was a particularly good season with the team finishing runners-up in the Lancashire League competition and finalists in the Lancashire Cup. In all, the team played some twenty matches, including four on a tour to Tyneside, winning twelve, losing seven and drawing one.

Although the Primary Town teams were still running, it is fair to say that at inter-school level things were not going all that well. It was left to only a handful of teachers to organise the local league and cup competitions. On top of that, some schools were failing to complete fixtures and others were just not turning up to play. In addition the withdrawal of some primary schools from the leagues made it easy to see the disenchantment of the Primary Association.

Despite splitting the Football Association into two separate bodies - a Primary Association and a Secondary Association - in the hope that this would help the junior schools, things did not improve. Unfortunately in the 1989/90 report of the Primary Association it stated that only the same three or four teachers were attending the committee meetings. Yet fixtures were still being organised, although by this time there had been a gradual shift to small-sided football and there were now three 7-a-side leagues as well as 6 and 5-a-side indoor tournaments. There was now only one 11-a-side league and a knock-out competition for the Jubilee Shield.

This was in stark contrast to the Secondary Association, where inter-school games continued to go from strength to strength and with a league and cup programme for each year group, boys in secondary schools were getting a better deal than ever before. Moreover, the successful local schools were then able to represent the Blackburn and Darwen Association in various Lancashire and English schools' competitions.

For example the 5th year team from Pleckgate in season 1980/81 were the Lancashire representatives in the E.S.F.A. United Biscuits competition. They had

Longshaw Junior School, winners of the Jubilee Shield in 1987. *Back*: P.Haworth, P.Egan, M.Douthwaite, L.Carroll, E.VanVessem, A.Gardner, N.Bond, B.Rush. *Front*: J.Hamilton, M.Eccles, C.Holland, M.Guittard, P.Westwell. The captain, Chris Holland, is the only Blackburn & Darwen schoolboy to attend the F.A. National School at Lilleshall.

Meadowhead Junior School, who shared the Thornton Shield with Shadsworth after draw-ing 0-0 in 1987. *Back*: D.Shepherd, G.Rose, C.Davies, M.Collinson, C.Slater, J.Neville. *Front*: A.Milligan, C.Berry, K.Cain, S.McPhee, I.Holt, S.Waddington, S.Keane.

St.Andrew's C.E. Junior School, winners of the Frank Littlewood Cup for 7-a-side teams in 1987. *Back*: C,Mercer, D.Trevelyan, D.Sutton, W.Riley, L.Davies. *Front*: D.Ratcliffe, R.Riding (captain), L.Flynn.

St.Peter's R.C. School, Mill Hill, winners of three trophies in 1989, the Primary League, the 6-a-side competition and the Jubilee Shield. *Back*: B.Willacy, G.Bolton, P.Ansbro, M.Davies, G.Williams, M.Leeming, S.Hargreaves. *Front*: S.Cowling, P.Greaves, B.Heggarty (capt.), L.Hamer, C.Ingham, L.Smith.

St.Gabriel's Junior School, winners of the Thornton Shield in 1989. *Back*: J.Read, S.Emery, M.Denby, A.Taylor, M.Riley, A.Walton, M.Cook, M.Lavery. *Front*: P.Sharples, A.Eaves, A.Kenny, A.Foster, S.Edmundson.

St.Bartholomew's C.E. Primary School 7-a-side team from 1988/89 and featuring the grandsons of two ex-Rovers - Bryan Douglas and Bill Eckersley. *Back*: Michael Douglas, Ben O'Hare, Christopher Wells, Billy Eckersley, Mark Schofield. *Front*: Brett Duxbury, Darren Tierney, Jonathan Carus.

won seven games to reach this stage before being eliminated by the Cumbrian champions in the first round of the national competition. Likewise in the following year, Darwen Vale 5th years won the Lancashire Schools' Open Cup competition for under-16 sides.

However, it was Town team football that really flourished, largely under the guidance of Secretary Mike Hodkinson and the various managers. It was 'Hodge' that built up a comprehensive fixture list for Blackburn and Darwen Town teams and as well as the competitive matches for the under-14 and under-15 sides, teams from all year groups travelled to play friendly matches against the likes of Leeds, Huddersfield, Bradford and Sheffield. There were even tours up to the North-East to play various Town teams in that region.

A good example was the 1989/90 season when the under-19 side played six games, the under-15 team 27 games, the under-14's 29 games, the under-13's 16 games and the under-12's played 7 games. It was during this season that the Secondary Town team progressed into a new era. A small band of dedicated teachers were determined to remould the Association at Town team level. Basically their aims were to generate enough money for teams to be smart on the field, to travel to away matches in the appropriate manner and to be generous hosts to all their visitors.

Within one year the influx of parents onto a Blackburn and Darwen Parents Committee saw the setting up of a system that made the Town teams financially

Pleckgate's most successful school team - winners of the league and cup double from 1981 to 1985, and winners of the Coldstream Cup in 1984. *Back*: Arschid Hussain, John Bentley, Steve Taylor, Mark Houldsworth, Paul Noel, Matt Gregory, Stephen Kay, Graeme Salt, Mohammed Hanif. *Front*: Andy Dickinson, Paul Howard, Mr.C.Smith, Mr.K.Walmsley (headmaster), Mr.G.Waddicor, Gary Brooks, Richard Stevens.

Some of the successful Darwen Vale teams with their trophies in May 1988.

stable for years to come. This was achieved through sponsorship deals, raffles and a Sportsman's Dinner which featured Jack Charlton, then the Republic of Ireland manager. It was a huge success, making a profit of £3,200. The following year the Parents' Committee raised £1,000 from a Sportsman's Dinner featuring Dennis Law and £700 from a raffle.

Within the first two years the Parents' Committee were able to provide new kits for five teams and meet the expenses needed to run five Town teams with a large fixture list; for example in season 1990/91 transport and catering alone cost £2262. Sponsorship played a big part in meeting financial costs and the Association was grateful to several organisations for their involvement, especially to Training 2000 who became the main sponsors at this time.

The Football Committee was honoured with two international matches during the 1980s. In 1983 the Football Association, through the English Schools' F.A., asked the Blackburn and Darwen Football Committee to stage a U.E.F.A. under-16 international game between England and Iceland at Ewood Park.

Although this was at very short notice, the local Association, under the chairmanship of John Duckworth and with the help of Treasurer George Crowther and Secretaries Mike Hodkinson, Mike Jackman and Peter Hopwood, did an excellent job. England ran out easy winners of the match but their side did contain several future stars including Tony Adams, Darren Beckford, John Beresford, Franz Carr, Dale Gordon, Kevin Keen and Tim Flowers.

In 1988 the local Association was asked to stage the English Schools' F.A. under-18 team versus a Dutch F.A. under-18 team. Whereas the English side were all schoolboys, the Dutch team were all attached to professional clubs and were a true national team. Not surprisingly they beat the English team quite comfortably.

The Blackburn and Darwen Football Committee once again showed it was more than capable of taking on the organisation of an international and the Match Secretary, Brian Woodhead, brought a flair for publicity and round the clock effort to the job. Other specific and important tasks were carried out by Gary Strickleton, Mike Hodkinson, Kevin Dobson and Chairman Pete Briggs. Over 4,000 people came out to watch the game on an icy cold night in early March.

While the influence of the Parents' Committee had a major impact on secondary Town team football, the influx of money did not, of course, guarantee success on the field.

Season 1992/93 was a particularly good year with success at both under-14 and under-15 level. This was also the first year that Bob Brownlee from Darwen Vale School took on the role of Secretary for the Town teams as Mike Hodkinson had to vacate the position when he joined the Council of the English Schools' F.A. It is ironic that in this first year the Town teams won three major trophies, almost as many as 'Hodge' had seen in the previous 17 years.

The under-14 team reached three finals, winning two and losing one. In the Divisional Final for the Woodward Cup at Burden Park they played well but were narrowly beaten 3-2 by a strong Liverpool team. However, they did beat Burnley 2-1 at the Anchor Ground to win the Wrennal Cup and they also won the final of the Granada Cup which was played at Pleasington.

The successful Under-15 Town Team of 1992/93, winners of the Lancashire Cup and the Alder Cup. *Back*: Mr.Andy Buckingham, James Beattie, Tommy Anderson, Ian Duerden, Kieran Hickey, James Webster, Phil Eastwood, Gareth Brown, Mr.Gary Strickleton. *Front*: Andy Margerison, Michael Peterson, Danny McNally, Danny Allwood, Chris Riley, Mark Canary, Simon Breakell.

The Junior Town Team of 1991/92 after they had beaten Lancaster 3-2 to clinch the Lancashire County Primary School League title. The team had remained unbeaten all season but, unfortunately, this was to be the last Junior Town Team. *Back*: Lee Gough, Mr.Phil Gardner, Andrew Dickinson, John Garner, Ian Zarac, Michael Preston, Leigh Monaghan, Mr.John Hacking, Nicholas Simpson. *Front*: David Hogan, Lee Dunleavy, Adam Norse, Paul Rowlands, Anthony Harwood, Andrew Preston, Nicholas Knight.

The under-15 side, under the management of Andy Buckingham and Gary Strickleton, had a wonderful season. Although they lost six out of their first seven games, the team then went through the rest of the season without a defeat, a run of 17 games of which they won 15 and drew 2. They became Lancashire Champions by beating Hyndburn in the final 2-1 after extra time. This game was played at Stanley Park, Blackpool. Even more impressive was the win in the final of the Alder Cup when the local lads beat Liverpool 2-1 on the Anchor Ground, Darwen. Liverpool were the English Schools' Trophy winners at the time and this was only the second occasion that Blackburn and Darwen had won this Cup since 1978.

From this excellent Town team, five players joined league clubs. Phil Eastwood, Ian Duerden and James Webster went to Burnley, James Beattie joined Blackburn Rovers and Daniel McNally went to Bury.

One other player who emerged from this era was Chris Holland, formerly of Longshaw Junior School and Darwen Vale. In 1991 Chris became the only Blackburn and Darwen schoolboy to be selected to attend the F.A. National School at Lilleshall. This school invites only the cream of schoolboy talent to spend their last two years of compulsory education there and Chris was in fact just one of 16 chosen. He joined Preston North End on leaving Lilleshall before being transferred to Newcastle United and is a member of the England under-21 squad. Perhaps one or more of these will make their mark in the professional game in the years to come.

The 1990s sees schoolboy football in a healthy state. There are plenty of inter-school matches at both junior and secondary level and standards of behaviour and play are very high. The Secondary Town team have more money and more games than ever before and have an excellent reputation both locally and throughout the North of England.

Success has continued over the last few years, with Darwen Vale under-16 team qualifying to represent Lancashire in the E.S.F.A. Trophy competition in 1991 and again in 1995. In fact, the team of 1991 reached the last sixteen of this national competition, defeating schools from Leeds and Chester on the way.

In 1995, the St.Wilfred's Year 8 team became Lancashire under-13 Champions, while the following year the Year 9 team of Our Lady's and St.John's School reached the final of the Lancashire under-14 competition.

The under-15 Town team of 1994 shared the Lancashire Cup, drawing 2-2 after extra time with Blackpool at Bloomfield Road. Managers of this team were Alan Cameron and Pete Briggs who both retired from Town team duties at the end of the season. They had been responsible for many outstanding Town teams and had given excellent service to schoolboy football over many years.

During the last 100 years teachers and schoolboy footballers have had to rely on the generosity of various individuals and organisations. For the major part of that time the Blackburn Schools' F.A. has been indebted to the directors of Blackburn Rovers F.C. for the use of Ewood Park for semi-finals, finals, county

St.Wilfred's Under-13 Team of 1994/95 who were winners of the Lancashire Under-13 Open Cup competition. *Back*: Mr.M.Dumbell, A.Connell, D.Shaw, P.Reeve, C.Ferguson, A.Whittaker, L.Tate, M.Pollard, S.Mills, Mr.S.Walker. *Front*: L.Varey, K.Sole, D.Leathert, S.Duckworth, A.Taylor, R.Rounding, J.Haydn.

games and international matches. Indeed thousands of schoolboys have experienced that special thrill of playing at Ewood and that feeling is something that stays in the memory for the rest of their lives.

Since amalgamation in 1974, Darwen F.C. have always been willing to allow the use of their ground for secondary finals and also for a number of English Trophy and Lancashire Cup games. Over the past twenty years, whether under the secretaryship of Jack Haworth, the chairmanship of Dennis Jepson or the managership of Ian McGarry, Blackburn and Darwen schools have always been made most welcome at the Anchor Ground.

The Football Committee has always had an excellent relationship with the local Referees' Society who have provided officials for semi-finals and finals for most of this century. More recently they have provided referees for local five-a-side tournaments and for individual schools who are involved in county competitions. Likewise, the local St. John's Ambulance Service has always been on hand at local finals and other important games to deal with any injury problems.

The Blackburn and Darwen Football Association owes a big debt of gratitude to all these organisations together with all the individuals who have donated trophies over the years, and more recently to all the firms who have provided financial support through sponsorship.

Over the past 100 years schoolboy football has developed and grown into what it is today. During that time the hundreds of thousands of children involved in

BLACKBURN
SHOPPING·CENTRE

Supporting

Blackburn & Darwen Schoolboy Football

Management Office
25 Church Street
Blackburn
BB1 5AF
Tel: 01254 54455

The Blackburn & Darwen Town Team of 1994 who were joint winners of the Lancashire Cup. *Back row from the left*: M.Emmett, I.Simpson, G.Haworth, G.Molyneux, D.Leonard, L.Jones, C.Connelly, P.Slater, A.Johnson, B.Duxbury. *Front*: M.Etherington, J.Fitzgerald, M.Douglas, C.Sutton, L.Slater, M.Krupa, C.Hunt, A.Smith.

football have been, for the most part, a credit to themselves, their teams and their schools. This is due in no small way to the thousands of dedicated teachers who have given up their time willingly and freely to make the past 100 years such a wonderful success. Blackburn and Darwen is such a football-mad area that I trust schoolboy football will continue for many more years to come.

COBBLE

The market leader in the manufacture of carpet tufting machinery

Cobble Blackburn are pleased to support the Blackburn and Darwen Schools Football Association

Cobble Blackburn Limited, Gate Street, Blackburn, BB1 3AH
Telephone: (0254) 55121 Telex: 63159 COBBLE G
Cable: COBBLETUFT Fax: (0254) 671125

Appendix I

Winners of the Harry Boyle Cup (Blackburn Schoolboys Cup) 1898-1996

Year	Winner	Year	Winner
1897/98	Parish Higher Grade	1948	Technical High School
1899	Emmanuel	1949	Audley Secondary Modern
1900	Emmanuel	1950	St.Peter's C.E. Secondary
1901	Emmanuel	1951	St.Mary's College
1902	Emmanuel	1952	Audley Secondary Modern
1903	Emmanuel	1953	Technical High School
1904	St.Stephen's	1954	Blakey Moor Secondary Modern
1905	Moss Street	1955	St.Peter's C.E. Secondary
1906	Emmanuel	1956	Technical High School
1907	Moss Street	1957	St.Peter's C.E. Secondary
1908	St.Philip's	1958	St.Peter's C.E. Secondary
1909	Emmanuel	1959	Technical and Grammar School
1910	St.Stephen's	1960	St.Peter's C.E. Secondary
1911	Moss Street	1961	Technical and Grammar School
1912	Christ Church	1962	St.Mary's College
1913	Christ Church	1963	Queen Elizabeths Grammar School
1914	Emmanuel	1964	Witton Park School
1915	Moss Street	1965	St.Mary's College
1916	Parish Higher Grade	1966	Billinge Grammar School
1917	Parish Higher Grade	1967	Billinge Grammar School
1918	Higher Elementary	1968	Billinge Grammar School
1919	Parish Higher Grade	1969	Billinge Grammar School
1920	Parish Higher Grade	1970	St.Mary's College
1921	Church of England Central	1971	Shadsworth School
1922	Church of England Central	1972	St.Mary's College
1923	Blakey Moor Central	1973	St.Edmund Arrowsmith
1924	Moss Street	1974	St.Mary's College
1925	Emmanuel	1975	John Rigby School
1926	Park Road	1976	St.Mary's College
1927	St.Aidan's	1977	St.Mary's College
1928	St.Aidan's	1978	St.Mary's College
1929	Moss Street	1979	St.Wilfred's High School
1930	St.Peter's R.C. School	1980	St.Mary's College
1931	Moss Street	1981	Moorland School
1932	Moss Street	1982	Everton School
1933	St,Peter's R.C. School	1983	Pleckgate School
1934	St.Andrew's	1984	Pleckgate School
1935	St.Peter's R.C./St.Thomas' C.E.	1985	Queen Elizabeths Grammar School
1936	Mill Hill Congregational	1986	No Competition
1937	St.Peter's R.C. School	1987	Pleckgate School
1938	St.Peter's R.C. School	1988	Queen Elizabeths Grammar School
1939	Emmanuel	1989	Darwen Vale School
1940	Blakey Moor Central School	1990	Darwen Vale School
1941	St.Peter's C.E. Secondary	1991	Queens Park High School
1942	Audley Council Seniors	1992	Queens Park High School
1943	Blakey Moor Seniors	1993	Queen Elizabeths Grammar School
1944	Blakey Moor Seniors	1994	St.Bede's High School
1945	Junior Technical School	1995	St.Bede's High School
1946	St.Peter's C.E. Secondary School	1996	St.Bede's High School
1947	Blakey Moor Secondary Modern		

Appendix II

Blackburn boys who have played for Lancashire Schools Under-15 Team

1921	Barnes
1922	Hargreaves
1923	Bilsborough, Duxbury, Earnshaw, Fisher, Hargreaves
1925	Earnshaw
1926	Standen
1927	Hosker, Thompson, Shuttleworth, Kay
1931	Holding
1934	Barrett
1935	Cowell
1936	Waywell
1937	Blake
1939	Sharples, Williamson, Cook (also England Schoolboys)
1947	Robinson, Wareing (also England Schoolboys)
1950	Spink
1951	Neville, Ingham
1952	Miller, Adcroft
1956	Pickering
1957	Fletcher, Ratcliffe
1958	Holding (son of Holding in 1931)
1960	Tomlinson
1962	Livesey, Kendall
1963	Holden
1964	Gillibrand, Harwood
1965	Metcalfe
1966	Isherwood
1967	Isherwood
1969	O'Neill
1972	Higgins

Lancashire reorganised into 11 Associations in 1974

1975	Duxbury (capt.), Wilkshire, Betts, Grunshaw, Hecker
1976	Moran (capt.), Caton
1977	Leeming, Smith, Brown
1978	Keough, Singleton
1979	Hanson, Lightbown, Procter
1980	Patterson, Walsh, Greenhalgh, Kasperowicz, Woods
1981	Brennan (capt.), Dunlop, Houldworth, Bennett, McCrae, Young
1982	Young, Breddy, Duckworth, Chapman, Rourke, Chadwick
1983	Watson, Knowles, Wilson
1984	Dickinson
1986	Smith, Blow, Taylor
1987	Haworth, Gallagher, Smalley
1988	Beattie, McHugh
1989	McGarry
1990	Haworth, Peake, Moss
1991	Leeming (capt.)
1992	Gaston, Woods
1993	Duerden
1994	Simpson, Connolly, Sutton, Hunt, Leonard, Smith

Lancashire changed from Under-15 to Under-16 Team

1995	Simpson, Connolley, Sutton, Slater
1996	Turner, Zarac, Jones

Appendix III

Blackburn Schoolboys who have played professional football.

It is difficult to list all the Blackburn Schoolboys who have gone on to play professional football over the past one hundred years, mainly because they are not recorded anywhere. Joseph Lofthouse, born in 1865, attended Blackburn Grammar School in the late 1870s and made his debut for the Rovers in 1892, making 83 appearances. Similarly, Bob Crompton went to Moss Street School prior to the start of organised football in Blackburn schools and went on to play 576 games for Rovers between 1896 and 1920.

Other early players who were born and bred in Blackburn and played professionally would include:-

Arthur Cowell
William Townley
Richard Walmsley
Harry Dennison (Blackburn Grammar)
Joseph Duckworth (Moss Street)
Thomas Baxter (C.E.Central)
William Wood
Harold Readett (Blakey Moor)
Hacking (St.Aidan's)
Walter Crook (St.Aidan's & Blakey Moor)
Leslie Cook (Blakey Moor)
Harry Healless (St.Bartholomew's)
Harold Jackson
James Baldwin
Tom Keaton

John Eastham (St.Peter's)
Albert Walmsley
Tom Riley
Arthur Edge (Blackburn Grammar)
Thomas Byrom
Wilfred Crompton (Parish Higher Grade)
Chad Townley
Spink (St.Aidan's & Blackburn Grammar)
Walsh (St.Andrew's)
Jack Chew (C.E.Central)
Verdi Godwin (Moss Street & Bangor Street)
Ronnie Haworth
Francis Chadwick
Tom Hargreaves

Since the Second World War the following have played professionally:-

Bryan Douglas (St.Bartholomew's & Blakey Moor)
Neil Ramsbottom (St.Stephen's Jun. & Audley Sec.)
Barrie Ratcliffe (St.James' Jun. & Tech. and Grammar)
Gary Talbot (Roe Lee Jun. & St.Peter's C.E. Sec. Mod.)
Alan Bradshaw (Audley Juniors & Q.E.G.S.)
John Byrom (St.Peter's C.E.Sec. Modern)
Roy Isherwood (Griffin C.E. & St.Peter's C.E. Sec.Mod.)
Neil Wilkinson (Witton Park)
Stuart Metcalfe (Witton Park)
Michael Duxbury (St.Mary's College)
Mark Brennan (St.Mary's College)
Peter Baah (Shadsworth)

John Waddington (St.Mary's College)
Harold Parker
Brian Miller (St.Mary's College)
John Airey
Derek Leaver
Fred Pickering (St.Peter's R.C.)
David Helliwell
John Kenyon (Emmanuel & Witton Park)
Paul Round (St.Edmund Arrowsmith)
Peter Devine (Witton Park)
Mark Patterson (Darwen Vale)
Steve Mullen (St.Thomas Aquinas)